GETTING RID
OF WHAT
YOU HAVEN'T GOT

Conversations
with Swami Muktananda

Published by S.Y.D.A. Foundation

Contents

About
Swami Muktananda

Swami Muktananda is a Guru. A Guru is one in whose presence the fruits of yoga are harvested. This is more than saying that he is a spiritual teacher whose instructions lead to fruitful results: it implies a "contagion" by means of which the benefits of spiritual practice are passed on directly, by presence alone. We are all aware of positive and negative influences in ordinary human interaction: we may speak of being "turned on" or "brought down" by people, or we may say that someone has good or bad "vibes." Yet the dominant strain in our culture is rationalistic, and we tend to dismiss the term "blessing" as a figure of speech. In Eastern spiritual traditions, however, as well as in the Old and New Testaments, this is regarded as a subtle energy—called grace, *baraka, shakti*—which the man of God radiates or may intentionally bestow, and which can effectively transform one's life.

Swami Muktananda has described in his book, *Play of Consciousness*, how he attained Self-realization by the grace of his own Guru, Bhagavan Nityananda. The path he has trod is, in turn, that which he recommends and makes available to his followers. It involved, in addition to exposure to the Guru's presence (in *darshans* and *satsangs*), meditation upon the Guru and the cultivation of an attitude of devotion, openness, and service towards him, for it is the quality of an individual's relationship with the Guru and the measure of his love which determine his ability to absorb the Guru's influence.

After centuries of kingship no longer parental and parenthood no longer divine, our culture has gone the natural pendulum swing into democracy and cautious anti-authoritarianism. The fact that Christianity itself is an embodiment of the devotional path only further contributes to our lack of receptivity, for it has often exposed us to deadened rituals, exploited faith, and the perversion of devotion into fanaticism. Thus we are prone to look upon personal reverence towards teachers and Gurus as immature, suspect, and even a bit embarrassing.

However, counterfeit gold exists only because real gold exists. Real Gurus do exist. So does *bhakti* yoga, a functional rather than merely sentimental form of devotionalism, i.e., one which constitutes a path of human development rather than a substitute for growth and, thus, a source of stagnation. One aspect of this yoga is that it prompts relating to reality as a Divine Being, which is to say a "Thou" or a person (rather than an "it" or an object) who is therefore endowed with qualities such as love, will, and intelligence. Another aspect is one that historical Christianity affirms in the case of Jesus Christ but (in contrast to other religions) denies in that of all other beings: the acknowledgement of an identification between the individual human mind and divine and universal consciousness. Whereas the West treats such identification with the divine as a taboo, the East looks upon God-realization as the mark of complete Self-realization and the goal of human growth. Since such is the claim of a *sadguru* (a perfect master), it is natural that love of God be projected upon him and that the relationship with the divine be cultivated through the relationship with him. The Indian tradition thus affirms of its *sadgurus* what Christianity affirms of Jesus: that the way to the Father is through the Son.

Even if we are not ready to accept the idea that man can reach divine consciousness or that God the Father has had more than a single Son, I believe we may agree that consciousness may be helped along its path by other members of His Family. The goal of the path that Swami Muktananda espouses involves turning one's devotion back from the Guru to one's own Self. "God dwells within you as you."

Swami Muktananda is certainly one of the great figures of India's spirituality of today. His activity is of particular interest in that it is not a form or a system of religious technology but is, rather, the art of soul-gardening.

Claudio Naranjo
Albany, California

The Necklace
Was Never Lost

People who come to greet Baba Muktananda never know whether they will be brushed by a peacock feather wand, crowned with a knitted hat, or sent away with a brusque wave. In this spontaneous way, Muktananda responds to every situation he is in; he is rarely predictable, always appropriate.

At the beginning of Baba's second visit to the United States, he gave a characteristically impromptu talk to a group of EST teachers in California.

Muktananda's talks always stay close to his own experience and to that of his listeners. When he teaches, the subtlest lessons of the Vedas and other traditional texts become simple, and filled with gaiety and graspable wisdom. His are not dry lectures on Hindu philosophy, but a broad poetry of the spirit.

What do you want me to speak about? Or, shall I say whatever comes to mind? You know, I have always been very fond of spending time with saints. As a young man I wandered from one saint to another, and there were as many as forty great saints in India at that time. I have also been fond of reading the poetry of medieval and ancient saints, because their words embody very subtle truths about spiritual life.

Knowledge is infinite, without any bounds, and how much knowledge you receive depends on how limited or expanded you are. This knowledge shapes itself to your needs. One of the most distinguished of the many saints India has produced, Jnaneshwar, who was supremely enlightened, says in a verse of his poetry: "Why don't you enjoy the state in which the mind completely extinguishes itself? Where the mind dissolves, the Self arises. Where 'science' ends, true knowledge begins." Jnaneshwar goes on to say: "That which remains after the mind has dissolved is present in all the states of consciousness: it's a pity you don't experience it."

The most important question raised in Vedantic philosophy is this: Can you attain what you haven't attained, or do you attain what you already have? If you are going to get something which you didn't have before, what good is it? Since you didn't have it before and get it now, there is every possibility that you'll lose it some time. And the question of getting what you already have is ridiculous, isn't it?

The truth is that we get what we have already got, not what we haven't got. We get rid of what is not—what we don't have—not what we have. This is Vedantic philosophy in its subtle and highest form. In Vedantic philosophy there is nothing to be done; the only important thing is understanding. Through understanding comes liberation.

A great philosopher-sage of our country, Shankaracharya, says in a Sanskrit verse: "The Self or soul is always present, it has always been there and will always be there; it is wrong to think that you got it just a while ago or will get it after you have done some spiritual practices." But, though the Self is eternally present within us, it appears as though it were not present, because we do not understand it and are not aware of it.

First we have to overcome our wrong idea. (I won't use the term "*maya*" which is translated as "illusion" because illusion is itself an illusion: it doesn't exist. And I won't use the term "ignorance," because ignorance is as unreal as illusion.) I say that we are not aware. We have made a mistake, as a result of which we don't achieve awareness of what is already there. Once we rectify our mistake, we will experience what we already are.

One day a woman was taking a bath in her tub on the first floor. As she was bathing, a procession happened to pass by along the road below her window. The procession was quite splendid, and the moment this woman heard the music she got out of her bathtub, dressed herself, put on all of her makeup, and came out to watch it go by. There were a lot of beautiful young women in the procession, wearing lovely rings and bracelets and necklaces. Sometimes, when you look at what a person wears, you think of a similar ornament you may be wearing. If you look at somebody's watch, for example, you have an impulse to look at your own watch. So, when she saw the other women's necklaces, she wanted to feel her own necklace, which was very expensive and made of diamonds. She felt around her neck and was shocked to find that the necklace was not there. She stood in front of a mirror and checked again—the necklace was not around her neck. She was shocked and began to scream, "Help, help, my necklace has been stolen, my necklace has been stolen!" Women from the neighborhood rushed to help, asking her what had happened. She said, "My diamond necklace has been stolen!" They looked for the necklace all over the place, in this corner, in that corner, in this corner, in that corner, and it wasn't anywhere to be found. Then one clever woman asked her, "Where was the necklace the last time you saw it?" She said, "It was around my neck," and touching her chest, she could feel the necklace. She exclaimed, "Look, here it is! It was hidden under my sweater." And she was happy; she had found the necklace.

The fact is that the necklace was never lost, and it was never found. The false outcry was raised: "My necklace is lost, my necklace is lost!" And then a squeal of delight: "It has been found, it has been found!" But the necklace was never lost.

Don't think we are any better than that woman. We look all over the place for the Self which is always present within. We look here and there, and there, and there. We look for inner consciousness, or we look for inner spaces in things which are outside us, and when we don't find them where they are not, we feel disappointed. The necklace was never lost, and it was never found. The Self has always been there. No matter where you are, you can experience the Self as it has always been, *right here and now*. This is the awareness of subtle philosophical truths.

An Upanishadic seer urges man to see the One who illuminates the three ordinary states of consciousness: waking, dream, and deep sleep. There is a seer within who keeps watching all that happens during your waking state. It's quite obvious that the seer is always different from the seen. For instance, at this moment I see one of you in the room where I am giving this talk, so I am different from him. And he sees me, so he is different from me. Just as one who sees a pot lying in front of him can never be the pot and is always separate from the pot, in the same way one who perceives the body separately, distinctly, can never be the body and is different from the body. We say, "my tape recorder," "my microphone," "my towel," "my hands," "my head," "my chest," "my stomach," "my legs." Well, they are *mine*, but they are not *me*. During the waking state we enjoy ourselves in different ways, eating and drinking, and giving and taking, and going and returning, and so on, but the one who keeps on watching whatever we do is different from all the activities we are engaged in. Then there is the next step, the dream state, during which you are asleep. The inner witness remains aware whether you are sleeping or not, and it's also aware of the fact that you have started dreaming as well as of the different things—all the strange events—you see in the dream world while staying separate from all of them. When you wake up, someone inside you tells you, "Look, you saw an elephant in a dream, or you saw a horse; you saw yourself crying, or you saw yourself laughing."

Another poet-saint says: "O Man, look within, go into your own inner spaces, and you will see that the Self, the light of the Self, is reflected through the intellect." You will also realize that you are not the body, that you are not a separate entity, that you are something else. We should try to find out who is the seer, the observer, the knower of the waking state and the dream state; who remains separate from them while watching them; and who exists within. That is the highest truth. Anyone who experiences that truth, that truth as "I," as "I am That," becomes that very truth. Compared to this understanding, all spiritual practices are futile. Practices have a secondary place. The first place is occupied by knowledge, by this understanding, and it's enough just to hear it.

There was a king called Janaka who used to sit on the bank of a river every day and practice awareness of the inner Self, continually repeating *So'ham So'ham So'ham*—That am I, That am I, That am I. There was also a great sage called Ashtavakra who, though he was just a young boy, was fully enlightened. Ashtavakra happened to pass by the spot where Janaka was sitting repeating *So'ham So'ham So'ham*. The boy was surprised. He said to himself, "Look at this! The king is supposed to be enlightened, yet like a kindergarten baby he is repeating *So'ham So'ham So'ham.*" He sat down in front of the king, holding his water bowl in one hand and a *yogdanda*, a T-shaped stick on which yogis recline, and he began to do his own mantra. But his mantra was not *So'ham*, not *Om* either. Neither was it *Om Namah Shivaya* nor *Radha-Krishna.* He began to repeat, "This is my water bowl, this is my yoga stick, this is my water bowl, this is my yoga stick, this is my water bowl, this is my yoga stick."

The king opened his eyes and saw a nuisance sitting right in front of him in flesh and blood. He said to himself, "I am trying to contemplate God, and here is a fellow who comes and starts indulging in his own brand of *japa*. I left the capital far behind and sought this solitary spot to get away from all disturbances and noises, but even here they seem to be chasing after me."

When Ashtavakra saw that the king was getting upset, he began to shout even louder, "This is my water bowl! This is my yoga stick! This is my water bowl! This is my yoga stick!" Janaka was so upset that he stopped doing his *japa* and he said, "O brother, what are you doing?" And the boy said, "You royal ass, what are you doing?" The king answered, "I am doing *So'ham So'ham So'ham.*

"I am also uttering a truth," replied Ashtavakra: "This is my water bowl, this is my yoga stick." Janaka, the king, said, "You holy ass, you don't seem to understand anything. Who says the water bowl is not yours? Why do you have to shout at the top of your lungs?" And Ashtavakra snapped back: "O King, it doesn't matter if I am a young boy. I

can be forgiven for my stupidity, but you are supposed to be intelligent, enlightened. Who has told you that you are not That, that you are not *So'ham*, that you are not the highest truth—so what's the use of repeating it like a moron?" Immediately the veil was lifted. The king got up and hugged the boy, and said, "You haven't been a nuisance. On the contrary, you have done me the greatest kindness."

The fact is that the truth always exists, and we always have, already have, the Self within us. If it did not exist within us now, it would not be real, because something is real only if it exists all the time. This is something which one should try to grasp through refined intelligence. Anyone whose intellect has been refined can know the truth directly within himself. There is another poet saint who sings, "Why are you looking for Him by wandering from forest to forest and mountain to mountain and temple to temple and place to place? Because He is right within you." *Alakh* is a word which means the invisible or impalpable, that which cannot be perceived by the mind or the intellect or the ego or the imagination. It is present in your heart; you have only to look there and you will see it, as you see your reflection in a mirror, as clearly as that.

One looks for it in the East, another the West, but none is able to find it, because to find it you need a Guru who can show it to you and explain it to you. Without a Guru you can't perceive it. Manpuri says that the Lord is within—why do you wander from place to place in search of Him? This is Vedanta. It is Vedanta in its purest form, the philosophy called *ajatavada*. Another poet-saint says, "There is a great mystery which I cannot figure out: though the Lord is within everyone, yet we do not experience Him." God's light can actually be seen. Whether you are confronted with unity or diversity, you must remain aware that the same one being has become diverse, and you will be able to realize this truth if you can see within. Know that to be the supreme deity. He dwells right within your body, just as bubbles dwell in water.

Manpuri says that the Lord is within your body and yet you wander from place to place in search of Him. (It's just like somebody holding a child in his lap, who sends a town crier around to announce that the child has been lost.) So Manpuri says that God dwells right within your body, and yet you are seeking Him from place to place.

There was another ecstatic saint called Mansur Mastana. He used to soar in the inner spaces, and he saw the highest truth right there. He began to say, "*Analhaq, analhaq*, I am God, I am God, the truth is within me, the truth is within me, I am in the midst of truth, and the truth is in my midst!" He began to dance. "I have found it, I have found it, I have got it, I have got it!" The orthodox clerics, who never understand a thing, got after him accusing him of uttering blasphemous heresy, and Mansur said, "I do not mean to utter heresy. I am only speaking the truth which I have experienced directly. From that, an understanding has spontaneously arisen within: I am not this body; I am that same divine light of which the whole cosmos is an extension." He continued, "You may break a mosque, you may break a temple, you may break any other holy place, but you must not break the human heart, because there the Lord Himself dwells. Inside a temple you worship an idol, inside a mosque you worship the void, but in the temple of the heart the divine light is scintillating, sparkling all the time, and that is the true house of the Lord."

Because he said this, he was hanged, and he proclaimed the same truth even from the hanging noose. From there he began to shout: "Down with all priests, down with all scriptures. Fling them into water. Go around proclaiming fearlessly, 'I am God, I am God, I am God!' Mansur Mastana says, 'I have recognized my true Master in my own heart.' "

Mantra Yoga

During the time Baba Muktananda spends in the United States, he teaches Siddha Yoga at retreats and intensives all over the country. The men and women who meet with Muktananda at these times leave their daily habits behind and, for hours each day, do little else but chant the names of God, meditate, and experience the words and presence of the saint from Ganeshpuri.

The passage of energy between Muktananda and the seekers occurs so quickly that by the second morning of a retreat or intensive many have received the transmission of energy known as shaktipat, and Muktananda's grace can be palpably felt as it flows through the people and atmosphere.

Muktananda takes special delight in the art of the intensive. It is a two-day vehicle of concentrated spiritual practices which carries the seeker inwards, closer to the Self. Whenever someone expresses doubt to Muktananda about whether he or she can learn to meditate — whether he or she is eligible to receive shaktipat — *he tells him or her, "Come to an intensive."*

He gave the following talk about the use and importance of mantra at one of his early retreats. Afterwards he told a devotee: "You won't find most of what I talked about today in any book. This comes out of my experiences."

This morning I shall speak on mantra yoga. Mantra is Maheshwara. Maheshwara is the great Lord, the supreme Lord, the inner Self, the all-pervasive Being. The mantra is the root of everything that we do in this world. It is the root of our practical dealings, of devotion, of yoga, of knowledge, of research in the spiritual.

The yoga of mantra is a complete yoga in itself. There are two aspects of mantra yoga. The first, called *swadhyaya*, is literally the study of your own inner Self. It also means chanting. In the morning at our ashram, at retreats, and in our homes we recite the *Guru Gita*, a hymn to the Guru, and that is nothing but the study of the nature of our own inner Self. The second aspect of mantra yoga is *ishwar pranidhan*. *Ishwar pranidhan* means to surrender yourself to the Lord in every possible way, to give everything to Him.

Your spiritual life, and your mundane life, are possible because of language—that is, words and sounds. The letters of the alphabet are combined into words, and the words are combined into sentences. We are able to function in daily life through sentences which express meaning. What a sentence is going to achieve depends on the meaning it conveys. Language comes from God. A verse says that God originally manifested Himself as sound, or as language. The mantra is also language; it is a combination of letters. The letters of the alphabet are combined into chants, the chants that we sing.

It is necessary to understand at this stage the real nature of mantra. Is mantra an ordinary combination of letters, or something more? It has been said that the mantra *is* the Lord, the highest being. The whole secret of mantra realization is that the mantra, the one who repeats the mantra, and the deity toward the realization of whom the mantra is directed are not separate from each other. They are one. Unless we become aware of this truth, we cannot realize the full power of mantra. The root of spiritual enlightenment is this knowledge of the true nature of mantra.

Language has tremendous power. A word, which we can call a mantra, can make you aware of something which exists at a great distance. If we use the mantra "Washington," a mundane mantra, all of a sudden the image of the city is conjured up in our mind, in spite of the fact that we may be thousands of miles away from Washington. The same is true of a spiritual word or mantra; it enables us to realize the Lord. We use a mantra for *shaktipat*: the Guru enters a disciple through mantra. The mantra that is quite often used is *Guru Om, Guru Om, Guru Om.* We must be aware of the meaning of mantra. If we are not aware of the meaning of mantra we keep changing it, as we change our hotels or our hair styles or our clothes.

Commenting on the misuse of mantra, a poet-saint said, "Everybody repeats the name of Rama, including cheats and thieves and priests." But the way that the great devotees such as Prahlad and Dhruva repeated Rama's name was entirely different, because that redeemed them. How did these great devotees realize the power of mantra? The answer is found in the *Shivasutras*, the basic philosophical text of the Kashmir school of Shaivism. In the *Shivasutras* there is a verse: "Unless you are aware that the goal or deity of your mantra is your own inner Self, the supreme Lord, you cannot realize the full power of mantra, no matter how much you repeat it. Only if you are aware of the goal of mantra will it bear fruit quickly. Without your being aware of its meaning, the mantra will not bear fruit at all."

There was another great saint called Eknath Maharaj who, it is said, had the beatific vision of the personal aspect of the Lord. He says, "Have the name on your lips and liberation in your hand."

If you want to go somewhere and a sentry is posted there who tells you, "No entry," you come back. This is the power of a mantra. "No entry" is like a mantra.

The fact is, every single word is a mantra, and every single letter is a mantra, whether we use it in our worldly life or in our spiritual life. If in the course of a discussion with a friend you become angry with him and you shout at him, "Shut up!", your friend goes away. His button has been pushed. Then, when you realize that you have annoyed your friend, you feel remorse, and perhaps you say, "I am sorry. I love you. I didn't mean to offend you." First you had pushed the wrong button; now that you have pushed the right button your friend becomes reconciled to you once again. From this you can see how much power words have.

Om is the primal word, the sound from which everything else has emanated. That sound was uttered in the beginning of the universe. *So'ham* comes from *Om*, and so has everything else in this universe. You find mantra, the word which was in the beginning, being echoed in every single thing in this universe including ourselves, but we are not aware of it.

Take, for instance, flowing water. When water flows it makes a murmuring sound. That murmuring sound is its spiritual language, or its mantra. It seems to remember God through that sound. Take the wind, rustling through leaves; the rustling of the wind is also mantra; by rustling, the wind remembers its creator. When we walk on the earth, our footsteps produce sound, and that is the mantra which the earth is repeating all the time to thank its creator. Space is constantly reverberating with sound. I have read the life stories of so many saints, and I have read in those stories quite frequently that they heard a voice coming from space, the voice of the heavens giving them a message.

Kabir, the great poet, says in his poems: "The Guru awakened me within by imparting to me just one word." Because we are not aware of the true nature of language, of the true nature of mantra, we get split up into different sects and cults, each one claiming a mantra for his own cult, and we keep fighting, to no purpose whatever. Though this globe has been divided into fragments which we call India and Europe and America and Pakistan, the fact is they are parts of the same earth. The water I used to drink in India is the same as the water I drink here. There was nothing especially Indian about the water I drank there, nor is there anything especially American about the water I drink here. But we like to apply labels. We eat the same food, we wear the same clothes, our clothes are made from the same cotton; our language also refers to the same objects. We may use the word "jala" for what you call "water"; but the difference is in the language, not in the object denoted by language.

Our concern should be meaning, not just language. I said that every single word has its effect instantaneously. Why can't a holy word have its effect instantaneously? The answer is that we accept a term of swearing, and we believe in it, while we do not believe in a holy word. That's why a holy word does not produce its effect. All the mantras which you find in various scriptures are quite true. The mantra scripture is quite scientific. If you were to repeat the mantra in the right way, it would not take much time to realize the mantra's power.

In our country, we hold very sacred rituals at which ritual mantras are recited. The priests recite the mantra, and we repeat it with them. There is a school in India which believes only in knowledge and condemns rituals. One follower of this school happened to pass by a place where a ritual was being held. He heard the priests uttering mantras, and he said, "What can you ever achieve by all this babble? It doesn't mean anything!" The mantra priest was very clever, and he said, "You stupid ass, get out of here!" The moment the fellow heard himself called this, he reacted. His mouth fell open, his hair began to bristle, his body started shaking, and he broke into a sweat. Then the priest asked, "Brother, what has happened?" The fellow replied, "You claim to be a priest, yet you have uttered such a phrase as 'stupid ass.'" The priest said, "Well, look at this. You have reacted so violently to what I said. I used just one phrase, a term of swearing, and it had such an impact on you. What makes you think that these holy words won't have any effect?"

I read a verse which says, "Mantra is true, worship is true, and God is true. You will realize their truth when you yourself become true." When you accept the truth of God and of mantra and of yourself, then poison turns into nectar.

The mantra is always obtained from the mantra seer, whom we call the Guru. A mantra, to be invested with consciousness, must be alive: it must be living. It should be taken from one who has himself fully realized its power. If you get a mantra from one who hasn't realized its power himself, how can it help you?

And who is a mantra *drashta*, a mantra seer? A mantra seer is one who received the mantra from his Guru and practiced it intensely. As a result, the mantra has passed with him from the physical level of speech to the subtle, causal, and supracausal levels. All the parts of his being are completely cleansed and purified by the mantra, and finally enable him to have a vision of the blue pearl, which is the supreme witness of the mantra that you practice.

Such a one is a mantra *drashta*, or a mantra seer. When you receive a mantra from such a one, it is a conscious mantra, a living mantra. It carries the power of the one from whom you receive it. It will bear fruit within you.

There was a great queen in our country who was named Mirabai. She was a great devotee of Krishna. Every morning she would sing hymns to Lord Krishna. She would wear anklets and dance in ecstasy, singing "Radha Krishna, Gopal Krishna, Radha Krishna, Gopal Krishna, Radha Krishna, Gopal Krishna." Her family, the royal family, did not like it, because they were all intoxicated by power and wealth; they were stupid asses. They couldn't bear that the queen of the royal household was repeating the name of this stranger called Krishna. They thought it was below their dignity for one of their ladies to be uttering Krishna's name, although they never thought it below their dignity to use the foulest language on every single pretext. They tried to argue with her, but she would not listen, because she had realized Krishna within herself. They gave her poison to drink, and she drank it, singing the name of Krishna. The poison turned into nectar; it would not kill her.

I will quote from Eknath Maharaj, a great devotee of Krishna, who says, "How can I describe the power of God's name? If you were to repeat it, God would reveal himself within you." The name has tremendous power. It is divine yoga, and, whatever people want to achieve, they can achieve it by repeating the name. They can get all the power they seek. In *Play of Consciousness* you must have read my description of the four bodies. Corresponding to those four bodies there are four tongues, or what you may call four levels of speech; and your mantra must pass from one level to another. In the initial stage we repeat the mantra with our lips or with the physical tongue. But if our mantra just remains there it will not bear much fruit. It must pass from there to a lower tongue, to the subtler levels of speech.

First you repeat the mantra, which you have received from a mantra seer. You repeat it on the tip of your tongue, and it vibrates there for a while. If you do it with sufficient reverence and love, then it will quickly pass to the throat center, which is the next level.

I am disclosing the mystery of mantra yoga, which has been a secret.

Once the mantra passes from the tip of the tongue to the throat center, it passes from the physical body to the subtle body, from the physical tongue to the subtle tongue, from *vaikhari* (the physical level of speech) to *madhyama* (the subtle level of speech). As the mantra descends deeper, its power also increases. The fruit, the reward which you may get by repeating the mantra on the tip of the physical tongue one hundred thousand times is the same as repeating it just once in the throat center. If your mantra is *Om Namah Shivaya*, you feel its vibrations in the throat center; there need be no response from the tip of the tongue. The mantra begins to fill you with gladness, and it makes you more conscious; it seems to renew and regenerate you. Your intellect is

also refined, and you begin to understand things, have new insights.

When the mantra begins to vibrate in the throat center, you acquire a marvelous healing power. However, you must not be swept off your feet by these minor miraculous powers; otherwise your further progress would be impeded. Swami Ram Tirtha says that a *siddhi*, or a psychic power, is a most terrible enchantress. My Baba, my Guru, had a whole mountain of *siddhis*, but he didn't touch it, though all the *siddhis*, all the powers, were working for him on their own. Nor do I ever touch any of these miraculous powers.

Once I read a story by Swami Ram Tirtha, who was a very great saint. There was a princess who was a terrific runner. She would run at tremendous speeds and like to race with princes. When she was of marriageable age, she laid down this condition: anyone who wanted to marry her should engage in a running contest with her, and if he defeated her, she would accept him as her husband. But if any prince lost the race, he would have to serve her as a slave for the rest of his life. Quite a few princes who were proud of their manly strength came and raced with her. Forty or fifty of them came, and every single one of them lost the race. As a result they were all serving her as slaves. Some would sweep her floors, others would fan her, others cooked for her, still others performed other chores for her. Now, there was one very clever prince who decided to have a race with the princess. He was very serious about it. He really wanted to marry her, and he also wanted to release all the princes who were in servitude to her. So he went to his Guru and asked him what he should do to defeat the princess in a race. The race was to cover three miles. The Guru said, "I'll tell you a trick. You should make about twenty-five gold bricks and before you begin the race make sure that those bricks are laid at an interval of a furlong each."

In the morning the race started. In the first furlong the princess was ahead of the prince. But when she reached the end of the first furlong, she saw the first gold brick and paused to pick it up. In the meantime the prince ran ahead. Then again she ran fast and left the prince behind; but at the end of the second furlong she saw the second gold brick and paused to pick it up. This went on and on. The prince left her far behind and reached the destination quickly, while the princess remained busy gathering all these gold bricks. She had quite a load to carry on her head. When the princess reached the destination, she accepted defeat and agreed to marry the prince. The prince got all his gold bricks back and in the bargain got the princess for his wife. He also got the fifty princes. All the wealth which had passed to this princess, all the wealth of the fifty princes—this too he got.

Thus, one who is running a race to reach the Lord should not have his attention distracted by the gold bricks on the path. If you are tempted by the gold bricks, you may never reach the destination, and you will be carrying a tremendous load on your back.

When the mantra reaches the second stage, the throat, many powers are manifested. One of them is that whatever you utter turns out to be true. It is then that you really begin to enjoy the name. The name becomes so enjoyable that one likes to repeat it all the time; and the name can be repeated no matter what you're doing, whether you're working, or playing with your children, or dealing with your wife.

Then the name descends from the throat center to the heart center, the third, or causal, level of speech. The deeper the *japa* goes, the more powerful it becomes. I told you that one repetition in the throat center is equal to one hundred thousand repetitions on the tip of the tongue. But one repetition in the heart center is equivalent to one hundred thousand repetitions in the throat center. One begins to go into a *tandra* state, a state of higher consciousness, and begins to have true visions, visions of gods and goddesses; and one also sees the deity of the mantra. Then he can see past and future, but he doesn't take any interest in that, because his interest is focused on the mantra itself. You can feel the vibrations of the mantra in all these centers. When a nerve begins to vibrate you can feel it. Similarly, if the mantra begins to vibrate in the heart center, you will feel its vibrations there.

From the heart center the mantra descends to the navel center. This is the fourth level of speech, the supra-causal level. Here you have the beatific vision. You become aware of the true nature of this universe, and you see God. It's difficult to say what boons God will grant to an individual who has reached this plane. He could be granted the boon of poetic power, or he could be granted the boon of saying something which is bound to come true. This is the mystery of the mantra. Furthermore, when the mantra begins to vibrate in the navel center, even when you are asleep you can hear the mantra going on within.

There is a special room in the ashram at Ganeshpuri which I always keep locked. There is no money in it; all the money is with the trustees. It is the room where I did *japa* and meditated for a long time, when my Guru was in his physical form. I did intense *japa*, as a result of which I realized something. That's why the mantra I give is able to awaken the dormant *shakti* of anyone. One day a high Indian civil service officer came over and began to express skepticism about the power of mantra. I said, "Why are you talking so much? There is a room of mine, I'll put you in there. I won't give you a mantra, but if you just spend time there you will be able to hear every single atom of that room uttering the mantra." So I sent him there. After he sat there for a while he began to hear *Om Namah Shivaya* coming from every direction. *Om Namah Shivaya, Om Namah Shivaya, Om Namah Shivaya*, even from

the walls. He broke into a sweat and rushed out of the room. He said, "O Muktananda Swami, O Muktananda Swami, O Muktananda Swami." His name was Dallal, and I said, "Dallal sahib, what has happened?" He said, "Well, the most amazing thing has happened. I heard your walls saying the mantra—now I just can't get rid of it. I can hear the mantra from my right arm, I can hear the mantra from my left arm, I can hear the mantra everywhere."

Such is the power of mantra. Mantra is a living force. No matter what object you strike, it will produce a sound, and that sound is its mantra. Therefore, keep repeating your mantra without interruption. This is a most simple and easy and natural yoga, which you can combine with your daily commitments. This yoga will fill you with peace and joy and love and bliss. Eknath Maharaj used to sing that mantra has tremendous power, asking, "Why don't you repeat it with absolute one-pointed devotion?" He said, "It will explode in your heart and reveal the bliss which lies dormant there." As you repeat the mantra, you will begin to hear the true vibration at the source of the mind, which is "*Om, Om, Om.*" *Om* gave rise to *So'ham*, and from *So'ham* the entire alphabet emerged.

Just as mundane mantras bear their fruit in your mundane life, spiritual mantras are bound to bear their fruit in your spiritual life. Mantra is absolutely true. Keep repeating it. Repeat the mantra being fully aware that the mantra *Om Namah Shivaya*, or *Guru Om*, as well as you who are reciting the mantra, as well as the lord or deity of the mantra—all these three are one. Then the mantra will give you realization quickly. As you repeat the mantra, you become one with the goal of the mantra.

There was a poet who has given expression to the power of mantra. He told how the supreme beloved of Krishna, who was called Radha, used to repeat "Krishna, Krishna, Krishna" all the time. She became so completely absorbed in Krishna while she was repeating "Krishna, Krishna, Krishna" that she began to ask her companions, "Where is Radha? Where is Radha?"

Sadgurunath Maharaj ki Jai. Meditate on your Self, honor and worship your inner Self, kneel to your Self, because the Lord of mantra lives within you as you. Compel him to reveal himself to you.

Thank you. I love you.

The Guru

Early every morning at Muktananda's ashrams in India and all over the world, devotees spend forty-five minutes chanting the Guru Gita, an ancient classic which, if studied carefully, yields the subtle meaning of surrender to the Guru.

The Guru Gita is sung in Sanskrit, which Muktananda calls "the language of God." But the text is accompanied by a literal translation into English, which enables the devotee to absorb the ideas expressed by the chant.

The role of the Guru may seem strange, even disconcerting, to Westerners. The sight of people bowing in reverence to a human being and the fact that this human being accepts such homage while sitting on a throne, seems degrading and dangerous to many. Frequently, people come to meet Muktananda, but refuse to bow. Or, if they do bow, they feel awkward and resentful about it. The question, therefore, is: why are we bowing, and who are we bowing to? Is the Guru merely the outer human presence that we see? Or is he something greater: an embodiment of some cosmic force—a mediator and reflection of our innermost selves? All of Muktananda's teaching is contained in the answers to these questions.

The best explanation of the Guru is his own presence. For those who haven't yet had the opportunity to be with Muktananda, this talk, which he gave at a retreat in the Santa Cruz mountains near San Francisco, provides a beginning.

Sadgurunath Maharaj ki Jai. This afternoon, this *yagna* of the meditation retreat will be consummated. I hope you understand the term "*yagna.*" *Yagna* is an elaborate fire ritual in India. This *yagna* is coming to its consummation in a smooth and beautiful manner. We have chanted and meditated a lot, and also listened to a lot of teachings about *kundalini* and yoga and mantra. Everybody has been quite peaceful, and many hearts have been opened up.

I have been asked to speak on "the guru." When I heard this request it surprised even me. Because, since coming to America, I find that there are at least fifty per cent as many gurus in America as there are in India. Still, people want me to speak on the guru.

The guru is a commodity which sells at a fantastic price on the American market. You have crowds and crowds of gurus, and they have been watering down their disciplines to the point at which those disciplines just disappear. The result is that the guru has nothing to give, and the students receive nothing from him.

There are all kinds of gurus: one prescribes tantric techniques, a second gives you a mantra, a third gives philosopical discourses. Then you have the guru-merchants. And there are the gurus who teach the yoga of alcohol, and gurus who teach the yoga of promiscuity and the yoga of drugs. The gurus are getting richer and richer, and their students are poorer and poorer. Some of the Indian gurus, after coming here, have become four-armed gods. It's because the Americans are rather simple and credulous in this matter. So any guru is a smash hit here. But in the end everything will be all right because you've got beautiful hearts and a willingness to accept what a true Guru tells you. A large number of gurus have exported themselves to your country from India, because it's very difficult to survive as a guru in India. It is quite easy to be a guru here; so you find more and more gurus migrating to America.

I read a story of Laila and Majnu in a book by Swami Ram Tirtha. Laila is the Indian Juliet, and Majnu is the Indian Romeo. The story of Laila and Majnu is a well-known story, and they have become legendary figures. Majnu was quite young, the son of a washerman. Laila was a princess, daughter of the king of the land. One day, Majnu's father asked him to bring the royal laundry to the palace. He went there, and he happened to get a glimpse of Laila. As destiny would have it, he became completely intoxicated with love for her.

Majnu became almost crazy. He could not move from the spot where he had glimpsed Laila, and the palace guards had a hard time throwing him out of the palace. From then on, Majnu was totally immersed in Laila, his heart was filled with her, and all the time he was repeating the mantra "Alas Laila, alas, dear Laila, alas, my beloved." Instead of repeating, "*Narayana, Narayana*" or "*Shree Krishna, Govinda, Hare Murare,*" he could only repeat "Laila, Laila, Laila." Majnu got so completely absorbed in Laila that he forgot himself entirely. He forgot about the world, and people had to take care of him, had to feed him, and clothe him, for he was incapable of looking after himself. When Laila heard reports about Majnu's condition, which was caused by his love for her, she too was affected.

Laila lived on the top floor of the palace, and from there she would watch Majnu pacing the streets shouting, "Laila, Laila, Laila." She caught the same infection, and she started shouting, "Majnu, Majnu, Majnu." It was quite even: Majnu was meditating on Laila, and Laila was meditating on Majnu, and they lost consciousness of everything else in the world.

Though the whole thing had started with passion, gradually their love became more and more refined and absorbing, until finally it became completely purged of passion. Majnu was so possessed by the purity of this love that he transcended the sexual appetite, transcended the sense organs completely. He got into a state in which even if he were to see Laila standing in front of him he would not have recognized her, because he was completely absorbed in the purity of this inner love. There is something most beautiful about this love. Compared to it, physical love, even between husband and wife, is ugly—there is something unpleasant about it.

Pushpadantacharya, who was a great sage and who composed a marvelous hymn to Shiva, says that it's a pity people do not know the bliss of Self, for once you know the bliss of the Self and become immersed in it, you find the muck of sensuality absolutely tasteless. This is what happened to Majnu and Laila. They transcended the sensual pull completely and became absorbed in the purest form of each other. Majnu completely lost body-consciousness; his outer condition became pitiful. He could not eat, he could not drink, he wore rags, his head was bare.

People went to the king and reported Majnu's condition to him, saying, "Your majesty, Majnu has fallen into a most pitiful condition. Do something for him." The king's heart was touched; he issued a royal command saying that all the shopkeepers should provide to Majnu whatever he needed, and the bills should be sent to the royal treasury. Businessmen will be businessmen. Their only interest was making money at the expense of the king; they were not interested in looking after Majnu. So they started providing for Majnu quite extravagantly. Cloth merchants would give him a new *lungi* every day, and restauranteurs brought him far more bread than he could eat. The shoe merchants brought him new shoes every day, and all the bills were sent to the royal treasury.

There were some lazy fellows in the town who, when they saw what was happening with Majnu, thought: "There is nothing like being Majnu." They were bored with work, they were bored with studies, they were bored with offices and stores and factories. They thought, "If I could become a Majnu, I would get everything free." So they had a conference and said, "Look, what's the point of slaving our lives away to our parents or our teachers at the univesity, or to our bosses in offices? It's much better to become Majnu." So they decided to become Majnus. The number of Majnus began to swell. The businessmen were delighted when they saw the number of Majnus increasing, because all the bills were being sent to the king. If there was a fellow working at a job he didn't like, he would quit and become a Majnu. If there was a young boy who found his parents treating him too strictly, he would leave his home and become a Majnu. In this way the number of Majnus rose to a thousand. At the end of the month an account was taken of all the bills flooding into the treasury, and it was discovered that the expenditure on Majnus was to the tune of a million dollars.

The treasurer went to the king and complained, "Your majesty, I am afraid we can't meet all this expenditure, because the number of Majnus is constantly increasing, and it is costing the royal exchequer a million dollars a month." The king was unnerved; he didn't know what to do. He had decided to provide for just one Majnu, but now there were a thousand. So he called his prime minister and asked him what they should do. The prime minister said, "Your Majesty, you yourself are responsible. You issued the order that Majnu should be clothed and fed free, and now all the slobs of the town have become Majnus. Now they don't have to work. It suits them beautifully. Not only that, all these Majnus are saluted wherever they go. But don't worry, Your Majesty, I'll take care of it."

The prime minister called a press conference, and he also called the town crier. And the command was sent out that, on the fifteenth day of the month, all the Majnus would be hanged. The moment the phony Majnus heard this command, they all ran away. One threw his hat away, another threw his *lungi* away, and a third threw his shirt away. One ran away to Mexico, another to France, a third to Pakistan. And on the morning of the fifteenth of the month, they could find only one Majnu on the street, who was still crying, "Laila, Laila, Laila." He wasn't at all conscious of what had happened, or of the order issued by the king. He was the real one. Somebody went to Majnu and said, "Majnu, the king wants to see you. When can he come to visit you?" And Majnu said, "He can come whenever he likes, but he must come as Laila, because I don't see anyone else but Laila."

This is exactly what has happened on the yoga scene. You have lots of yogi Manjus appearing on the market, because to be a yogi is quite profitable. You get a lot of food, you are honored and respected, you can charge a fee, and you can pass off anything on credulous folks. If the American government were to pass a law against the yogis operating in this country they would all run away. Only the real one would remain: the one to whom the hanging noose means nothing. Therefore, even if you are on the spiritual path, you must keep your eyes open. You must be very careful, very alert, about where you are going and what you are doing.

When you go to a guru, first see if yoga has been absorbed into his own personality, and how much power of yoga he has. The other day a yogi met me. This yogi is quite respected, with quite a large following. He had a pot belly, and he said that he has been teaching yoga. I asked him whether he himself was practicing any yoga. And he said, "I gave that up long ago. Now I only teach it."

You find people teaching meditation who do not meditate. You find people teaching yoga who do not practice. A true Guru would not make things so cheap; he would not initiate people so easily. He would first test them thoroughly, before initiating them. Likewise, students should also test a Guru thoroughly before accepting him as their Guru. Anyone who claims to be a Guru must be totally disciplined. He must exercise self-control in food and drink, and in talking, and in every other thing. In fact, you should see the signs of yoga even in his body, in all the sense organs.

Who is a Guru? A Guru is one who has absorbed the divine power of grace into himself, and kept it alive in him, and who can dispense grace easily to all those who come in contact with him and who need it. A true Guru, through the practice of yoga, through philosophical or metaphysical contemplation, and through love for *his* Guru, succeeds in saturating even his physical form with the power of yoga. It is not only his inner Self which becomes one with the supreme Self; even his body becomes completely conscious, becomes completely spiritualized or divinized. The real Guru is one in every part of whose body you find rays of *chiti* blazing. In his presence, yoga comes to you naturally, spontaneously. The rays of *chiti*, the rays of divine energy, keep emanating from him all the time and passing into spiritual seekers. A Guru becomes like an advanced tuberculosis patient infested with TB germs—his clothes are filled with germs, and the food he eats and the water he drinks become infected. If anyone were to touch his body or his clothes, or drink the water he has tasted, he would catch the infection. Likewise, a Guru is completely saturated with the rays of *shakti*, or divine energy. You even find divine chiti flowing out through his breath. If he were to blow into someone's nostrils or eyes, chiti would pass into that person. And that person would catch the germs of yoga. His hats become saturated with chiti. If he were to throw his hat to somebody, rays of chiti would pass into that person. This is what a true Guru is like.

I am telling you the marks of a true Guru, and you must find out for yourself whether or not a particular guru you have encountered is a true Guru. Some of the marks are: his body becomes transmuted into pure energy; he can give *shaktipat*, awakening the dormant *shakti* of a disciple; he can remove all the blockages from one's nerves, opening up all the knots in personality and all the chakras, without any surgery; he is completely conscious of truth, completely aware of it, and can transmit truth directly to a disciple; he has completely mastered all the scriptures; he is established in supreme peace and experiences it without interruption; and he has mastered all his sense organs completely. His eyes will see only if he commands them to see. His hands will move only if he commands them to move. His tongue will speak if he commands it to speak. His mind will think only if he wants it to

think. And he has conquered all the six enemies, such as lust and wrath and greed and attachment and so on. These are the marks of a Guru. A Guru is not a con man who cheats his disciple of his wealth. A real Guru cheats his disciple of his suffering, of his misery.

If you stay in the presence of a true Guru, *sadhana* comes to you quite spontaneously. Just as you have self-propelled boats, the *sadhana* of a disciple becomes self-propelled. Once the Guru gets it going, it goes on and on by its own momentum. If you keep company with a true one, then you overcome bondage. You grow and expand until you become infinite, until you become the supreme Lord Himself. A Guru turns his disciples into God. A Guru rids a seeker of seeking, transmutes him into a Guru: he bestows Guruhood on disciples. He doesn't like to keep them as disciples forever. Such a one is alone worthy of worship. Such a one will be able to do a lot for you.

Another mark of a true Guru is that he rises constantly; he doesn't know any fall. He rises from this plane, and he keeps rising and rising and rising until he touches and becomes established on the highest place. A true Guru will not fall from a higher plane to a lower, nor will he struggle and writhe and wallow in the muck of the lower planes.

It is very difficult to recognize a true one. That is why it is essential for a seeker to be a true seeker, an ideal seeker, a real seeker. One should not be in a hurry to accept a Guru, because taking a Guru is the most significant, the most far-reaching event in your life. From birth to death you do so many things. You grow up and get married, you have children, you look after your family, and so many things happen to you. But entering into this Guru-disciple relationship, or accepting a Guru, is the most meaningful thing that could ever happen.

You don't have to run around in a rush to accept a Guru. Stay calm. Just make yourself a better and better disciple. I can assure you that there is a world of *siddhas* or Gurus, which I have visited, and which is full of real Gurus. If you become ready for it, a Guru will come from that abode of Gurus and initiate you from within. He knows how to initiate you. The moment you are ready he comes to know of it, because these Gurus carry radar which can detect a true disciple from any distance—the range of this radar is unlimited. The moment a true disciple comes into the presence of a true Guru, the Guru knows what to give him.

So you should stay calm and keep praying to the inner Guru, because the supreme Guru dwells within each one of you, and when the time is right, someone will come and initiate you. It happens in life that when a person begins to feel bored with himself, can't stand himself any longer, he goes and looks around for a partner in the hope of brightening up his life. But the partner turns out to be equally self-hating, and when these two come together, they only wind up hating each other more and making each other more and more miserable. Previously there was only one who was weeping; now they hug each other and weep together. They help each other in weeping more, not laughing more. This should not happen between a Guru and a disciple. When you get sick of suffering in this world, of agony, of all kinds of conflicts and tensions and anxieties, you turn to a guru in the hope that he will give you some relief. But what quite often happens is that the guru and disciple hug each other and weep together in their misery. The guru has nothing to give the disciple, and the disciple has nothing to give the guru. The guru hasn't seen Ram, and the disciple doesn't see Ram.

I read a story about King Henry of England. To fill his treasury, he thought of the device of awarding titles to people in return for money. He began to create lords and barons and dukes and knights and so forth. One man went to the king and said, "I, too, want a title." The king said, "I can give you any title. and the fee is such and such." The man said, "Give me the title of Guru." "No, no," said the king. "That I cannot do. Ask me for something else. I can create a duke, I can create a baron, but I can't create a Guru. I would have to be a Guru myself. You have to earn the title, you have to win the grace of a Guru and work very hard to become a Guru." Therefore, do not rush to accept a Guru. There is no hurry. First find out whether a particular guru is worthy of being a Guru; if he really has spiritual power, you may accept him. Always remember the inner Guru, the Guru who dwells forever within you, and he will certainly bestow his grace on you. You shouldn't worry or be anxious at all, because once you are worthy of having a Guru, God will certainly send you one.

I am very happy that all of us have spent three days here as one united, integrated family. I am sure you aren't going away from here empty-handed. You should be constantly aware of who you really are. There was a great spiritual philosopher in our country who studied all the scriptures that there were to study, and himself composed a large number of abstruse philosophical scriptures. Then, after finishing his elaborate work, he wrote one *sloka* in which he says: I am going to give you the essence of all the countless scriptures I have studied, of my entire experience of life, of all that I have seen and understood and known; it is this: The world is nothing but God. It is God who manifests as the countless forms and shapes which you see around you in this world. It is God who has become you; you are a perfect portion of the divine being.

This truth, that God is you, is even greater than the truth that the world is God. This is the awareness that you must not lose, even for a moment. There was a poet-saint in our country who says, "Where are you looking for God? He lives in every single cell of your body, in every single corpuscle." There is no other abode of God.

I have seen this truth in meditation with these very eyes. I have seen that inner light, that spiritual radiance, that blue glow spreading through all the nerves and giving dynamism to blood corpuscles, carrying them from one place to another. I am uttering pure truth with this very tongue. When by the grace of the Guru, by the power of *kundalini*, by the power of meditation, your consciousness expands, you will be able to see that divine light filling you from head to toe. You will see light illuminating every single corpuscle, every single molecule of flesh. Therefore, you must not slight yourself, you must not put yourself down. There is no greater sin than this. You must think nobly of yourself. You must learn to respect yourself. You must become aware of your own greatness, of your sublimity, of your own worth.

There was a seer called Manu who said: "Which sin has that thief not committed who has stolen all the glory from the Self?" In other words, there can be no worse sin than to remain ignorant of the glory of your own Self, considering yourself to be insecure, petty, a sinner. There could be no grosser insult than to neglect yourself. Be aware that Ram, the Lord, reposes in every single blood corpuscle. This is the Lord, who has been described in the scriptures: He is beyond the reach of the intellect and the senses, beyond the reach of the mind. He is unlimited, he is boundless. He cannot be seen by the physical eyes unless they have become completely refined by the Guru's grace, and then you can see Him with these very eyes. He is without beginning; He has always been. He is the One in whom all really good people, in whom all the spiritually evolved Gurus, repose, in whom they have their final rest.

The poet Tikanath composed a song that says: "By the grace of the Guru who dwells in my *sahasrara*, the Guru who is pure, who has no taint, by his grace I have become completely pure, and I have become totally blessed."

Sadgurunath Maharaj ki Jai! So think well of yourself. Why think ill of yourself? If you must think, well then, think: "I am the Self. I am pure love. I am a bubble in the ocean of God."

Sadgurunath Maharaj ki Jai! I thank everyone. I love you.

Turning a Prison
Into Paradise

One morning Wesley Zineski dropped in to see Baba Muktananda where he was staying in Piedmont, California. Zineski had an urgent desire to establish contact between Muktananda and the inmates of San Quentin State Prison, just across the bay from San Francisco.

Zineski is a quiet, middle-aged man who owns a coin-operated laundry in San Francisco. In his spare time he is a voluntary teacher at the school of religion run by the prison for its inmates.

He had hoped that Muktananda would be able to visit the prison school. But at that time San Quentin was in more violent turmoil than usual, and the acting warden had put out an order banning all visitors.

"I didn't want the men there to be deprived of Baba's message," said Zineski. So, when he visited Baba, he brought along a tape recorder. This is the message he was given . . .

There was a very great saint in Karnataka, the part of India I come from, who was an *avadhoot*. A false charge was brought against him, and he was thrown in prison. The authorities didn't realize that the man was innocent. He was imprisoned for six months, and during that period he transformed all the prisoners. He used to conduct great chants and sessions of meditation. Then the jailer realized that the charge against him was a false one and recommended in his report to the judge that the saint be released. They offered to release him, but he refused. He said, "I will go only after my sentence is complete, because here I have a wonderful opportunity to work with people, and here I enjoy solitude. It is not a prison to me. It is like a Himalayan cave where I can work on myself and work on others."

There are so many people sitting around me in my ashram, and as long as they are here they are in a kind of jail, because I insist they must not move or talk unnecessarily. They must read from their chanting books. If we want to pursue our *sadhana* effectively, we have to follow a

35

very strict discipline, the kind of discipline they insist on in a jail. We must get up early, we must go to sleep early.

Now, by God's grace, you so-called prisoners have a wonderful opportunity to devote yourselves to spiritual growth. All your time can be spent on spiritual growth. You should not consider the place where you are to be a prison. You should consider it a place where you can grow spiritually.

My dear prisoners, why don't you change your point of view? Instead of considering yourselves prisoners you should consider yourselves yogis who have chosen to be in a solitary place for the purpose of spiritual growth. Now you are living a disciplined life. You are away from all kinds of worldly involvements, and you can live your life in detachment and devotion. All of you should get together and chant *Hare Rama, Hare Rama, Rama Rama, Hare Hare, Hare Krishna, Hare Krishna, Krishna Krishna, Hare Hare*, and then this prison will turn into a paradise, and people outside the prison will want to come and live in your paradise. If I can find time, I will come and visit you.

You should remember that it is not easy to be born in human form. Human form is very special, it is very high, it is very noble, and you should be reflecting on why you have been born in human form and what the purpose of your life is. Our scriptures say that one should suffer the consequences of his past actions cheerfully. You are where you are because of certain actions of yours, and you should bear their consequences cheerfully, by devoting your time to chanting the divine name and meditating and remembering the Lord. Then, when you come out of the prison, people will realize that you have come out of a paradise.

I welcome all the prisoners with love. I love all of you.

The Value of Dying

Charles A. Garfield is a lecturer in psychology at the University of California, Berkeley. He has urgent, dark eyes that seem to strain to see beyond what is in front of them.

Unlike most of Muktananda's visitors, this young man had not come with questions about the quality of his own life. He heads a project at the UC Medical Center that is concerned with the difficulties of dying.

A few days after his interview, he wrote the ashram, saying, "Baba appears as an incarnate statement to Western psychology . . . that we are neophytes in the understanding of 'the play of consciousness.' "

Baba: What are your findings?

Charles: So far we have just been spending a lot of time with people who are dying. We haven't found out much yet.

Baba: It is very difficult to see exactly what is happening within a dying person at that time. You can only see what is happening outside, and how much shows? Departure from the body is an extremely subtle phenomenon which is very difficult to see. I was present at the deaths of three or four *siddhas*, or fully realized beings, and about five or six devotees, pure-souled people, and five or six people who had reached a state of even-mindedness.

If you want to get a direct and true insight into it, you will have to have your inner *shakti* awakened and meditate, because in meditation you can see your death at least once. That experience is worth having. Before a yogi has his final realization he can see a number of his past incarnations, from three to seven — what he was in his last life and what he was before that and so on.

Charles: Is there any way to help someone who is not a yogi?

Baba: There are two reasons why people suffer so much while

37

dying. One is inordinate greed, and the other is the memory of all the horrible deeds one has performed.

There was a great being, a fully realized being called Zipruanna, who was a great friend of mine. It was he who sent me to my Guru. He was fully aware of the past, present and future. He had great love for me. Over there is his picture. He licked me on the head. He used to stay completely naked and would live on a pile of filth. Though he was naked, dust or dirt didn't stick to his body. He could always see everything. School and college boys would follow him around and ask Zipruanna, "Will I get through my exam?" If he said yes, they certainly would, but if he said no, they would not. It was he who prophesied once that the time would come when people all over the world would get to know about me. When his final time came, a lot of people who loved him were around. One of them was an old teacher, a woman. He went to her home. He said, "Massage my body with oil and put some hot water on; I want to have a bath."

She massaged his body and gave him a bath and then gave him some milk. After he had drunk the milk he said, "Now Zipruanna is leaving, and you can cry as much as you want to." And he left his body.

That is how a yogi leaves his body. That was all that woman could see. She couldn't see what was happening inside of him, how he left his body or where he went after he left his body.

I will tell you about my own Guru. He was a great *siddha*. I worship his picture every day. One day I was worshipping his picture in my meditation room, and all of a sudden the frame broke into pieces. I came outside and told my men that Baba was going to depart. And he passed away within a fortnight. He would lie down anywhere—on the bare earth or on rocks—and the result was that he contracted very severe rheumatism or arthritis. His knees became locked and it was very difficult for him to walk. The evening before the day of his final departure, I came to know that he was going to pass away the next day. He was lying in his bed. A doctor was massaging his hands, and I was massaging his feet. I have a good knowledge of the various nerves in the body, and as I was massaging his legs, one of the nerves in his body stopped working, and his legs stretched straight out. The doctor let go of his hands, and I began to massage them. He opened his eyes quite wide and looked at everyone. Then his eyeballs went up and he made a snore-like sound and left his body. I was watching him very carefully, but that was all I could see. Before he died, he could not straighten out his legs, but at that time his legs were perfectly straight. Just before his death he overcame his arthritis. Our scriptures say that after you have suffered your bad karma or your bad destiny, that karma is exhausted, and I saw an example of it at that time. He had been suffering from arthritis for the last two or three years, but just at the time of his death his karma was exhausted, and he could stretch out his legs.

I have told you about two *siddhas*. Now I will tell you how a devotee died. He was a street hustler. He used to sell snacks, and he used to eat a lot of fish and drink a lot of alcohol. I was quite young, and I was doing my *sadhana* in Yeola where he lived. Three years before his death he gave up meat and drinking and began to remain immersed in thoughts of God all the time. He continually chanted *Narayana, Narayana, Jaya Govinda, Hare*, even while doing business or walking through the streets. He loved me very much and would bring me things to eat. In those days I lived in a house outside the village, but I would go to his place for my tea. Three years after he had become a devotee of God, he fell ill with fever. He called me and said, "I am going to die." We called a doctor, and I still distinctly remember his words when he saw the doctor. He said, "O Lord, why have you come? I know I am going to die. You can't save me."

That was Sunday. The following day he called me and his wife and said, "I am going to depart on Tuesday, and before I die my beard must be shaved off. Since it is Monday today, I won't have it shaved." (Monday is considered to be sacred to Shiva, and we don't shave our beards then.) On Tuesday his temperature came down and his beard was shaved off. He called for me and said, "I must have a bath." He was given a bath. He told everyone—I even jotted it down—"The messengers of God have come, and I will leave in a short while. I can see the messengers of Vishnu." At 11:00 A.M. he took just a small quantity of rice. He uttered "Hari, Hari, Hari," and that was the end. I saw that with my own eyes, and that image has now come again to me very vividly. I can see it even now. But what after that?

The first two were *siddhas*, so they died peacefully. This was a devotee, and he only told us that the messengers of God had come to take him away. The name of that devotee was Don, and everyone was amazed to see him die that way. He underwent tremendous transformation in three years. I have watched many people die. There was a time when I was very fond of watching how people died. Then I saw other people of other types die. Their death was extremely painful. They writhed and twisted with agony and passed a lot of shit when they died. According to our scriptures, that is a sign that they will go to hell.

Charles: Is there anything that a person who isn't enlightened can do to help someone die?

Baba: What can you possibly do at that time, the final time? As long as a person is still conscious, he should be made to turn to the divine name. Suppose somebody who has met with an accident is going to die and is restless: what can you do at that time? Way before death one should be urged to start remembering the Lord.

If you really want to know what is happening at that time, you should meditate. A yogi has an experience of his own death. That experience is most valuable. You can see your death very distinctly, and you can experience it fully. You can even see yourself depart—see the soul depart from your body—and you can see it move farther and farther away.

Charles: Are there any particular practices one can do to have that experience?

Baba: This experience comes of its own in an advanced stage of meditation. The inner *shakti*, the inner energy or *kundalini*, brings this experience of death. It is an experience worth having. There was a great poet-saint in India, Tukaram Maharaj. He says, "I saw my own death with my own eyes." I used to ponder these words quite often, wondering what they meant. Then I had an experience of my own death in meditation, and I realized the truth of his words. I saw my own death with my own eyes. It is possible to have such an experience.

Then there are quite a few people who are possessed and tormented by ghosts and evil spirits, the spirits of people who have died.

Charles: How is the victim chosen? How does that happen?

Baba: These ghosts and evil spirits live in subtle bodies. As far as choosing who to torment, a stupid ghost will get after anyone who comes his way. The other day while I was lecturing, a man from the audience seemed to get upset. He stood up and said, "You seem to be set upon turning people into God." He raised his arms and left the hall. If somebody were to ask him, "Why did you yell at that swami?," it would be difficult for him to answer. I would say that he happened to be there and he happened to choose me to be his victim. An evil spirit is a spirit which does not follow good reason.

The other day a boy came here who said, "I have been possessed by an evil spirit, and he is tormenting me very much."

I slapped him on his head. Then I gave him the mantra, asking him to repeat it. He returned after three days, and I asked him, "How are you?" He said, "I am no longer tormented." He was here just yesterday.

You can't usually see a ghost or an evil spirit; but there is one way, and that is to acquire a subtle eye through meditation. Through that eye you can see these subtle things.

Charles: In the West people are using psychedelic drugs to attain that kind of egoless state that people develop through meditation. Is it possible through these drugs?

Baba: That isn't so good. I can accept that by the power of drugs your awareness is compelled to turn within. It is just like injecting chloroform into the body and, for a while, the body is divested of consciousness. But it is different when the *kundalini* awakening takes place within a person. Then one goes into deep meditation, and in that state

the *shakti* eats up his ego and the person transcends his ego. You can get much higher than you ever get on psychedelic drugs. Meditation does not have any adverse effect on the body or mind. On the contrary, it whips up the fire of digestion and purifies other inner organs and lends new vigor and liveliness to the mind, making it more refined and subtle.

Charles: I understand the difference in healthy people. What about people who are dying and who haven't practiced meditating? What about using drugs with those who are dying?

Baba: What is the effect of the drugs on them?

Charles: It seems to promote a mystic-like state which seems near the egoless state. A person undergoes several of these experiences. Then the treatment is stopped and a person is left with a state of egoless-ness and dies more peacefully.

41

Baba: I have no objection to that. Since you are performing such experiments, only you know what the results are.

Charles: We are trying—it is very new.

Baba: What drugs do you give them?

Charles: LSD.

Baba: How long before death?

Charles: They have been using it with cancer patients who have maybe six or more months to live.

Baba: You should be able to find out the exact time of death. According to *ayurveda*, certain changes begin to take place in the body ten or fifteen days before a person's death. There are certain physicians in our country who are very intelligent, very clever, and who, just by feeling the pulse of a patient, are able to see that he is going to die within a certain amount of time.

Charles: That would be very valuable information. Is there any way I could find that out?

Baba: There are some experts who could teach you that in India—*ayurvedic* physicians. *Ayurveda* is the Indian system of medicine. You can make that prediction just by feeling the pulse of a patient. If you know the time of death of a person, it would certainly help a lot in your experiments. I have been given to understand that there are some good *ayurvedic* doctors who can get to know when a person is going to die.

Charles: In the West, doctors are not interested in that sort of information. They are very much afraid of death themselves.

Baba: A doctor will not tell the patient that he is going to die within two or three days, but he can come to know and he can tell the relatives. Supposing there is a person who is very weak. A doctor may say that there is no use performing an operation when he sees that a patient is going to die anyway.

Charles: I have heard that at the time of death a person is most open to the experience of enlightenment. Is there anything a person can do to help him attain that state?

Baba: When a person is dying in our country, friends and relatives come and chant *Hare Ram* or recite the *Gita*. We keep chanting even after a person has died until he is cremated. In India the divine name is used very much on these occasions. The dying man immediately clutches the divine name and gets rid of the fear of death because the divine name has so much power in it.

"I Have Become Everyone"

Baba Muktananda was interviewed by Susan Berman, a reporter for the San Francisco Examiner. Their talk ranged widely. Muktananda spoke frankly about his life, his aim in coming to America, and what it feels like to be the focus of so much intense feeling on the part of his followers. It shows a relaxed, human side of Muktananda's personality, which is moving to see and remember.

Susan: What is Swami Muktananda's basic message for the American people?

Baba: My message to the people all over the world, not only to the Americans, is: Meditate on your Self. Honor and worship your own Self. Kneel to your Self, because the supreme reality, the highest truth lives within you as you.

Through meditation the body becomes strong. Prana—respiratory rhythm—becomes calm and steady, and the intellect acquires a new strength. As a result, people can function more effectively in the world.

Susan: What made Swami Muktananda become a monk?

Baba: Right from my early life, I had been hearing about saints and God from my people at home. Then around the age of fifteen I happened to see a drama. The hero of that play was a young boy whose name was Dhruva. He was a child saint. As I watched him on the stage, I was very profoundly affected, and I left my home. I suddenly felt powerfully drawn towards the Lord.

Susan: How did you find your Guru?

Baba: While I was still in school my Guru happened to visit our school. He used to stay almost naked, except for a loincloth. When he visited a school, the boys would leave and follow him. He had great love for children. He would feed whatever anybody gave him to children. At that time he hugged me, and the result was that after a few days I left home. Then my Guru later settled in Ganeshpuri, a village about fifty

43

miles from Bombay. After leaving home, I kept wandering around India for years and years. In the course of time I also happened to visit Ganeshpuri. There I met my Guru again and he initiated me with *shaktipat*. That got me into meditation. He passed away in 1961.

Susan: How did Swami Muktananda become a God-realized being? How did he know? What was different about the feeling before and after?

Baba: If something happens to go wrong inside, you're immediately aware of it. In your present condition you are aware of your own state, what you are feeling, whether you are happy or unhappy, whether you feel good or bad. Likewise, when you realize God you become aware that you have realized Him. Also, there are lots of inner experiences which precede the final experience of God-realization. I meditated and meditated and meditated, and in the course of meditation I saw, in the thousand-petalled spiritual center in the crown of the head, a sun which was much brighter than the sun that you see outside—a dazzling brilliance. Then many other visions followed. As you have these visions, knowledge or understanding of them arises from within. You become spontaneously aware that you have seen the highest truth. Truth has the power of making itself known to you and also making you aware that you have known it. Take the sun for example: it not only illuminates other things, but also itself.

Susan: What does Swami Muktananda think about the fact that he is so popular with Americans?

Baba: First, you know, I am popular with myself. And if you become popular with yourself, you become popular with others. Then, all those people who come to me are readily accepted by me. That is why people seem to like me very much. A couple of days ago I spoke in the Masonic Auditorium. There were seats for about 3,500, but about 4,000 people turned up there each night. After all, people seek what they like, what is dear to them, what they love. Don't you think everybody would like to be with one whom they love?

Susan: Is it difficult to live your life as a realized being?

Baba: No.

Susan: Is there anything you would rather be doing than teaching? You never have any desire to just be a regular person? To be anonymous?

Baba: What I am doing at present is something most important, and at this time anything less important would not have any appeal for me. No matter where I go, I will, after all, carry myself with me, whether I am in a forest or in the midst of multitudes. God has created such a vast world, and He is running it, and He never feels bored. He never thinks of running away to a mountain. So why should I abandon the multitudes and think of retiring into a solitary cave or a mountain? A lot of people live in the mountains. Some of them are natives of the mountains, but I don't see any evidence of tremendous evolution in them.

Susan: What is wrong with the world that we have wars and famine?

Baba: That is the way of the world. That is how the world goes. The main reason is egoism, or pride, the basic cause of man's selfishness.

Susan: I have never been around a saint before. What does he eat, how long does he sleep and does he have a chair like this at home in the ashram? In what style does he live at home?

Baba: I get up at 3 A.M., and have a cup of light tea. Then I have a bath, and afterwards I meditate. For quite a while I am absorbed in meditation on God. After sunrise I recite the *Guru Gita* with all my followers here. (Open the doors so that we can hear the chant going in the hall.) Then I receive visitors and talk to them. Then for lunch I have one plain vegetable and rice which is grown around Delhi. In the afternoon I have a little rest. I am talking now about my lifestyle back home. I also look after the ashram and attend to the various problems. Again I am available to visitors. Thousands of people visit the ashram, and thousands of them are fed there. After meeting visitors, when it is dark, I retire into my room and meditate again, and then I sleep for a while. There is not just one such chair, there are lots of such chairs in the ashram.

Susan: Why do you think that Americans are now so interested in Swami Muktananda and the whole Indian experience?

Baba: It is because through what I teach and the practice of yoga, one's body becomes strong, and one derives new inspiration for living one's normal life in the world and carrying out one's social responsibilities. Look at the girls here. Look at their glow. They don't even feel like drinking tea or coffee. For this reason the young people are turning to yoga. Look at these girls. See the love in their faces. For this reason they have turned to yoga.

Susan: How does Swami Muktananda's teaching differ from some of the other Indian leaders in the country, such as Maharishi Mahesh Yogi, and others?

Baba: My teaching could not be essentially different from the teaching of other Indian gurus. However, I emphasize meditation on your own inner Self. I don't exactly know what other gurus emphasize. After coming here, I haven't investigated it. I don't know what they ask their followers to meditate on. I ask my followers to meditate on their own real or true inner Self. The yoga of meditation is not a cult or any kind of religious politics appearing in a new form. Just as sleep is natural to everyone, so is meditation natural to everyone. Meditation lies just a little beyond sleep. Meditation is neither Hindu nor Islamic nor Christian nor Jewish. Meditation is the universal religion. It is the religion of every man, and every individual can follow it independently.

Susan: Do you think that America has a high spiritual place compared to India, or low, or in the middle?

Baba: I find tremendous interest in spirituality in America, and there are lots of people pursuing it. Indians like to describe their land as the land of spirituality, as the very home of spirituality. However, I am seeing a spiritual revolution all around me in this country. The Americans have already reached the moon. Inner peace comes next, and that is why they are now pursuing inner peace.

Susan: Do you think the spiritual revolution will come in my lifetime, or in many hundreds of years?

Baba: It doesn't take long. Spiritual evolution occurs very quickly. One generation has seen the emergence of atom bombs and hydrogen bombs and rockets. It would not take very long for people to turn within and find their true Self. Science and technology are leading people towards spirituality now. Besides, you people, you reporters, can spread this subject throughout the world in no time and get any number of people intersted in it.

Susan: Do you ever get lonely being a saint, like a king, exalted at the top?

Baba: I never feel lonely because I have become everyone. I never feel lonely because I consider the whole universe to be my own. When the entire cosmos is my friend, how can I feel lonely?

Susan: I have a deadline for tomorrow's paper. I have to go. I wish I could stay longer. Isn't there any other message you would like to give to the American people?

Baba: You can return whenever you have time. All that I have to say is that just as you have made progress in the material and scientific fields, you should now turn towards the inner Self and find real peace which dwells within. Then your life will become complete. The world and the spirit should go together. Let your life become permeated by yoga. This is my message.

Susan: Thank you very much. I think you are very nice. I enjoyed it very much.

Baba: You should come again when you have more time; maybe you would have a direct experience of inner peace. If you were to sit with me for one hour you would be right there, you would get within yourself and then you would write a very good story.

Susan: I can use it. We don't get much inner peace at the newspaper.

Shaktipat
Epilogue by Paul Zweig

When Paul Zweig visited Mukt-
ananda at the urging of an old friend,
he was totally unprepared for the ex-
perience of the Guru's presence. Much
later he said that he had always assumed
that human happiness was available
only to children and madmen, that no
sane adult aspired to happiness. But
when he met Muktananda, Zweig
said he tasted joy, and he tasted it not
as some forbidden fruit but as his own
forgotten birthright.

A noted author and chairman of
the Department of Comparative Lit-
erature at Queen's College in New
York, Zweig wrote the following ac-
count of his meeting with Muktananda
in his book, Three Journeys, *pub-*
lished by Basic Books in 1976.

I think of Walt Whitman sitting under an apple tree on Long Island, drunk with the odor of crushed grass. I think of William Blake conversing with angels, and Jakob Boehme cobbling God's shoes. I think of Plato's *Symposium*, describing the ladder of universal love as an ascending current of knowledge mingled with delight. In that conversation between drunken friends, the wisdom of East and West mingle playfully, preparing future marriages.

I think of my own experience not long ago, sitting in a strangely decorated room, the air perfumed with incense. At one end is a seat draped with richly colored cloths. On the walls hang several greatly enlarged photographs of a dark-skinned man in a loin cloth, his body oddly smooth and glowing, his face expressing a combination of sleepiness and alert attention.

A few days before, I had received a phone call from a friend I hadn't seen in quite some time.

"I've been in India for three-and-a-half years, living in an ashram," she announced, "and now I'm in New York for a while with my Guru. Why don't we get together?"

This was astounding news. Apparently my friend's life had taken some unexpected turns since I last saw her. I was embarrassed to admit I didn't know what an ashram was. My friend had gone to India to "shop around for a Guru," she explained jokingly, and after some looking had found one. I didn't exactly know what a Guru was, either. Gurus had something to do with the wisdom of the East, I remembered ironically. They were some sort of wise men you went to when you had a question. I concluded I would rather ask my friends, or read a book.

Nonetheless, I was here to check out Odile's Guru. We'd had coffee together the day before, and she'd talked about her life in India. She had always been a tough-minded person, and that hadn't changed. If anything, she seemed tougher now, almost ominously solid. Whatever she'd been up to, it had somehow accentuated her personality, so that there seemed to be a kind of overflow in her movements.

She spoke slowly, pausing for a long time between words. I had the impression she had never talked about these things before, and that stuck in my mind more than anything she said. What sort of experience, I wondered, could a strong-minded, intelligent woman have been engrossed in for three-and-a-half years, without ever having tried to explain it, even to herself? A few other things stuck in my mind. Her Guru, Swami Muktananda, wasn't simply a Guru; he was a *sadguru*, the highest level of Guru; so high, he had nothing in common with the pleasant-faced Indian gentlemen in white clothing one met presiding over yoga centers throughout America. A *sadguru* was something else entirely. Not simply a teacher, but a "perfectly realized human being." I heard that expression in quotation marks, because it didn't seem to me it could be used in any other way.

But Odile wasn't talking in quotation marks. "He's quite an unusual man," she said, smiling thoughtfully. "In India they call him a saint, but in a way, I think of him more as a warrior."

Muktananda's temporary ashram in New York was a lovely red brick school house near Riverside Park, where, I was told, he took long walks every day before dawn. Consistent with his aura of sainthood, he had never been mugged. In fact, the idea was vaguely humorous. Later I would have dreams of violent young men running up in the darkness to throw themselves at his feet. He would bend over and thump them on the back, or walk by, playfully raising his eyebrows.

I had been ushered into a medium-sized room with large windows, where a number of people were already waiting. The curls of burning incense, the colorful chair, the exotic paraphernalia; people sitting expertly in the lotus posture, or leaning against a wall, or gathering their legs about them as best they could: the atmosphere was low key, yet vaguely expectant. An air of dormant obsession pervaded the room, making me feel as if I ought to pay attention, though I had no idea to what.

I didn't see the door open. He was simply there, quite suddenly. He walked across the room and sat down with a series of quick, fluid movements. Odile had warned me that he wouldn't seem very holy, and she was right. He wore an orange ski cap, dark glasses, and a gaudy robe that looked as if someone had raided a costume store. On the whole he bore a slight resemblance to a jazz musician, except that his face had a kind of feathery alertness. He settled onto his chair, checked a clock, tapped a microphone to see if it worked, looked for a pile of orange cards on a side table, and sprinkled perfume on a wand of sumptuous peacock feathers. He seemed to be in perpetual motion, occasionally darting glances around the room at one person or another.

I had been startled when several people had touched their foreheads to the ground when he entered the room, but I didn't really pay much attention, mainly because I didn't feel concerned. I wasn't even there out of curiosity, I reminded myself, but simply as a gesture of friendship to Odile. I noticed that the man in the enlarged photographs on the wall was not Muktananda and asked Odile about it. She said the photographs were of Muktananda's Guru, Nityananda: a large-bodied, imposing figure, naked except for the loin cloth, and emanating a gruff, disturbing energy. He seemed quite different from the loudly dressed man moving around on his chair at the front of the room. There was a dank, almost demonic quality in the photograph, and a stillness which seemed to inhere in the figure itself.

Muktananda communicated through an interpreter, a lively young man dressed in orange robes, who sat cross-legged on the floor at his feet. The interpreter called the name of each visitor to come up and be introduced. Not much seemed to go into an introduction. You got to say your name and what you did, while Muktananda tilted his head graciously and smiled. His smile was crisp and restrained, yet benevolent in its way. However theatrical his clothes might be, Muktananda's face did not indulge in flourishes; on the contrary, even his wit had a quality of severity. My turn came early in the hour. I went up and, observing what appeared to be a practice, got on my knees while the introduction was made. Odile, to whom I had given copies of some books I had written, dumped them on the floor in front of Muktananda, who picked up the books and looked at them while the titles were translated. He asked if the word "emptiness" in one title had anything to do with the Buddhist void. I answered that I had never thought about it. Did I want to ask him anything? That was the furthest thing from my mind. I said no, and the introduction was over.

More people were introduced. For the most part they were younger and had been involved in the Oriental scene in one way or another. Some had qustions to ask about meditation; a few had been to India. The sort of questions they asked rubbed me the wrong way: they seemed full of melodrama and inflated romantic excitement. "Sometimes I feel within me . . ." "I know in my heart . . ." "My inner awareness . . ." "My cosmic feelings . . ." I moved over to get a better look at Muktananda. For all his quickness and sudden changes of expression, there was a kind of distance in his face, an immobility not unlike the face in the photograph.

A young woman was speaking to him. She had lived for several years in Pondicherry Ashram in India. She gave Muktananda a drawing she had done and in a high tremulous voice said she had a question to ask him. I found myself paying attention suddenly, not so much to what the woman said as to a feeling of vulnerability in her voice. When she meditated, the experience of silvery light was very intense, but then nightmarish forms came between her and the light, and she was frightened. Her voice became increasingly tenuous as she talked, and then it broke. I could tell she was crying. She had lifted up a hand, as if to describe the nightmares, and I saw that it was shaking. And suddenly I was shaking too. I felt as if I were rooted to the floor, trembling with intense feeling. I had to make an effort not to cry, yet it wasn't simply crying, for my body had become buoyant, warm. I stared at the woman's hand sketching a movement in the air: it was pale, delicate. Even after the hand was tucked away in her lap and Muktananda's voice had begun to speak an answer, I went on staring. My eyes seemed to be peering out of a deep, silvery tunnel, while the forms and colors of the room glided across their surface like paper cutouts.

The words, "afloat in tears," repeated themselves in my mind, and an overwhelming idea seized hold of me: all of us do our best against suffering and useless pain. Those nightmarish forms the woman had talked about were the element of my life, and everyone's life. All of us sitting in this room were on the point of crying out, for we existed far from the light. I had accomplished all sorts of things in my life. I had a position in the world; I wrote books; I was a discriminating person who cringed from the naive self-importance of these "kids." Yet nothing I had done meant a thing from the viewpoint of that light. I, too, was defenseless, full of longing; and we were equal, because we were human.

As I stared at Muktananda's quick movements, I became aware that my mouth was hanging open, but I couldn't seem to close it. For some reason I wasn't frightened; I was even pleased, though I couldn't say why. Muktananda had done this; but what had he done, and how? We hadn't talked much, and he had hardly looked at me. He was not especially charismatic: no great gestures or fixed, piercing glances. He moved around a lot and played with his fingers. All the while I was holding back my tears by an effort of subtle attention. The tears seeped onto my face anyway, a few at a time.

Later in the hour I managed to stand up and indicate that I had a question after all. I marvelled that my limbs still functioned as I made my way to the front of the room. The atmosphere was dreamlike and filmy, and I felt strangely dissolved in it.

"My question is the same one you asked me earlier. What *is* the connection between the experience of inner emptiness, the frightening feeling that at some level of my existence I'm nobody, that my identity has collapsed and, deep down, no one's there; what is the connection between this feeling, and the Buddhist void?"

"They are the same," he answered immediately, "but in the Buddhist void there is no fear."

Later on I thought about Muktananda's answer. But at the time I was too preoccupied with my emotional upheaval to think clearly at all. If anything, I felt vaguely disappointed, for what he said seemed like a non-answer. It was said off-handedly, too, not as one ought to speak to someone whose life was breaking into warm, tearful pieces. I felt ever so faintly rebuffed; yet I was moved, too. Until that very minute I had accepted mental pain as an ordinary part of life. I believed that my insufferable anxieties belonged to the fabric of existence; that in some way they were a good thing. This morning, sitting on a hard, wood floor, looking at a dark-skinned Indian man with a large belly and an orange ski cap, a strange light had been driven into my gloom: the sickness can be cured, it *has* been cured. You are already free. I was experiencing the delirium of release.

Toward the end of the hour, a nervous, red-headed man was introduced. He stood in front of Muktananda and began talking in a voice full of forced arrogance:

"You people talk of bliss and liberation, but you ought to know that you're a tiny minority, a mere fraction. Most people don't see things your way. They suffer, and they hate. They work, and they feel frustrated. That's reality. What would Anatole France say about you, I wonder?"

His body stiffened while he talked, and his shoulders hunched up defiantly. Every once in a while, he squeezed a laugh from his throat which resembled a cackle. He tried to get a cigarette to his mouth, but his hand was shaking too violently.

"What right do you have to announce that you're happy to people who are suffering? This is evil. Anyway, you can't prove it. How do I know you're not lying? You talk about love and compassion. You claim you're not afraid to die."

Baba cut in, "Just as you have the right to say you are unhappy and cling to your unhappiness, so I have the right to say I am happy. You love your unhappiness and I love my happiness."

He cackled again. Then, as if forcing himself to speak:

'Listen, I'm terrified of dying. What would you do if I pointed a gun at you right now, if I pulled a gun out of my pocket and pointed it at you?"

There was an undertone of violence in his voice that seemed almost crazy. Clearly the man was out of control; he might do anything, I thought. But Muktananda's interpreter did not seem at all nervous, although some visitors were getting ready to be scared, as I was. When the talk about the gun occurred, Muktananda answered:

"My love would still be coming toward you while you pulled the trigger."

I remember thinking: this is preposterous; no one can say such a thing and mean it. At the same time I was stunned by a thought which filled my mind: yes, it's possible; such a response is possible. For an instant I glimpsed depths gaping under and around the small island which I had confidently labelled human nature. I felt ignorant; yet my ignorance was filled with happiness, because it seemed to me that something previously inconceivable was not only possible, but was happening before my eyes. It's odd, but I didn't ask myself if Muktananda were telling the truth at that moment. I was too overwhelmed by my discovery to even think of such a question.

The red-headed man seemed to collapse. He threw his head back and laughed, almost shyly. All at once he was hugging himself and turning his body from side to side like a little boy. Everyone was laughing gently, and the man seemed vulnerable, lonely. His fingers were caked with nicotine, and they still shook a little. With his talk of Anatole France, he reminded me of an uncle of mine: a nervous, frustrated intellectual. He reminded me of myself, or an aspect of myself: a frail, wiry individual who couldn't afford to be truly generous, who needed all his energy simply to stand still, at all costs, including inner paralysis, as if he were a rim around nothing, and had to expend quantities of passion simply to maintain the integrity of this rim.

Muktananda glanced at a pop-art clock on the table beside him. He said something in Hindi to his interpreter and stood up, glancing around. The devotees bowed, and he walked briskly out of the room. His way of walking was unique, yet marvellous too. It would gradually become imprinted on my mind during the weeks that followed. He leaned backward a little and swung his arms in a long outward arc. This made his round soft stomach especially prominent. When I mentioned this to Odile one day, she smiled and said that it wasn't really a pot belly, but a result of breath-retention. Most of the great *siddhas* had round bellies. So did the Buddha.

After Muktananda left the room, we were invited downstairs and served lunch in what must have been an auditorium in the building's school days. I sat on the floor and thought the food into my mouth. When I wasn't thinking, my arms stopped, and a fullness heaved from some remote inner place, seeping out as tears. The people waiting for lunch chanted in a language I'd never heard before. Their chant was rhythmic and full-bodied, not at all like a church song or a religious hymn. It struck me that these people were having a good time. At the front of the room, a group played rhythmic accompaniment on a drum, a harmonium and a tall, twangy instrument. Their music fed the mysterious intensity which came and went, making my body seem roomy and full. I had no idea what was happening to me, but for some reason I still wasn't afraid, or even curious. I was simply absorbed, as if I were singing or dancing with complete abandon. Yet I was sitting completely still, my face expressionless. I might even have seemed sad to an observer.

I remember the afternoon in bits: trying to talk to people, but not able to say more than a few words before tears overwhelmed me; Muktananda's appearance a while later, wandering across the auditorium to his seat near the stage. I had become so absorbed in my experience it was a while before I noticed and hurried to sit near him, as did everyone else. Somehow he looked blacker, more solid. My eyes began to stare as they had that morning, tunneling deeply into themselves. Everything was so vivid: Muktananda's wiry, black beard and the moods flitting across his face; later, on my way home, the excruciating clarity of store windows, mounds of garbage, faces streaming toward me like separate pieces of a single awareness.

I remembered what a devotee had said to me during lunch: "It looks like you've got it."

What, I asked, had I got?

"*Shaktipat*, a dose of Baba's *shakti*, his energy. That's what you're feeling now. Baba says that all of existence is a play of *shakti*, but that our personal *shakti* is dormant, as it is in external objects. Being intensely aware of objects is equivalent to awakening the *shakti* in them. That's what Baba does. He activates the dormant energy in us. It's like a lamp being used to light another lamp."

The explanation didn't really make any sense to me. Merely to follow it as an actual explanation of something that happened, like the law of gravity, required a wrenching of my mental habits which was quite beyond me. Nonetheless, I was dumbfounded. Apparently other people had had this experience often enough to give it a name: *shaktipat*. This thought alone was full of wonder for me. I was experiencing something real, something with a name.

At that moment I glimpsed a mental trap I had lived in all my life. Despite being largely endowed with "inner resources," as the saying went, I had never fully accepted the reality of my feelings. An experience became real for me only when I shared it, giving it a name like tree, chair, or face. Without the name it remained a little dubious, a little undependable. All my life I had read books, studied them, eventually written them; and the point of my reading and writing had been a persistent, anxious quest which no quantity of written words could satisfy, but which the acts of reading and writing themselves appeased while they were being performed: the quest for words capable of communicating to me the reality of my own feelings. Adam named the animals according to a technique which had, apparently, been lost to me, for his animals stayed named, while mine sank back again instantly, so that nothing was ever gained except the experience of naming itself which, therefore, could never be finished, and also could never be wholly satisfying.

All my life I had been convinced that my character had condemned me to a sort of impurity; that, for example, I could never keep a secret because, in my system of identity, secrets became empty and unreal when I refused to speak them. They became a threat to my integrity because, when they dislocated in silence, I felt myself dislocating too. Secrets made me dizzy, and I did my best to avoid them, often by simple ignorance; I couldn't tell what I didn't know. The result was that I often knew nothing, especially about myself.

Even on that first day, walking home along Broadway in a state between dreamy relaxation and pure aerial energy, I sensed that my system had been overthrown, because what I was experiencing was irrefutable. This upheaval didn't need me to prove its reality. On the contrary, it was proving my reality, just as fear or erotic excitement are tremendous proofs of one's reality.

It occurred to me that I could keep this secret if I chose to. The energy fusing from every part of my body sufficed to itself. It wasn't so much beyond words as it was alongside of them, in some other realm. I liked that idea. In a confused way, it increased my feeling of self-respect. My life, it seemed, was no longer subject to the universal law of suffering. I had escaped by some miracle which I connected to a dark-skinned man in a ski cap, whose precise features, movements and voice already seemed a little blurry; for that very moment, walking, filling the sidewalk with my presence, was so much more real than any place I could be coming from or going toward.

Glossary

ashram   the dwelling of a Guru or saint; a spiritual community.

avadhoot   a renunciant who has risen above all concern for the world.

Baba   a term of affectionate respect meaning "father."

bhakti   love of God

blue pearl   the abode of the inner Self, seen in deep meditation.

chakras   six subtle centers through which the awakened *kundalini* rises.

chiti   divine conscious energy.

darshan   to see a saint is to have his darshan.

Gita   abbreviation for the *Bhagavad Gita*, a famous Hindu scripture.

japa   repetition of the divine name or mantra.

Kashmir Shaivism   the Indian school of philosophy which views the world as a concrete manifestation of consciousness.

kundalini   the spiritual energy which lies dormant within every individual and which, when awakened, initiates spiritual growth.

lungi   a traditional skirt, worn by Indian men

mantra   a sound with the power to transform one who repeats it.

sadguru   a true Guru

Sadgurunath Maharaj ki Jai   a phrase which means "Hail to the true Guru."

sadhana   spiritual disciplines or practices.

sahasrara   the center of consciousness in the crown of the head.

satsang   the company of saints and their devotees; a gathering of devotees.

shakti   power; divine conscious energy; also *chiti*.

shaktipat   the process by which the Guru's spiritual energy is transmitted into a seeker, thereby awakening his *kundalini shakti.*

siddha   a perfected master

Upanishads   ancient teachings, forming the final portion of the Hindu scriptures, the *Vedas.*

Vedanta   the Indian philosophy which views the world as a manifestation of *maya*, or illusion, veiling the consciousness which underlies it.

Other
Publications

Play Of Consciousness *Muktananda's Spiritual Autobiography*
Satsang With Baba *(Three Volumes) Questions and Answers*
Muktananda-Selected Essays *Edited by Paul Zweig*
Light On The Path *Essays On Siddha Yoga*
Sadgurunath Maharaj Ki Jaya *Photos and Essays Of The 1970
   Australian Tour*
Siddha Meditation *Commentaries On The Shiva Sutras*
Mukteshwari I & II *Aphorisms*
So'ham Japa *Short Essay On The So'ham Mantra*
Ashram Dharma *Essay On Ashram Life*
A Book For The Mind *Aphorisms On The Mind*
I Love You *Aphorisms On Love*
What Is An Intensive? *Description of Muktananda's 2-day program*
Bhagawan Nityananda *Biography Of Muktananda's Guru,
   Swami Nityananda*
Sadhana *Photographic Essay of Muktananda's Spiritual Practice*
Muktananda Siddha Guru *By Shankar*
Swami Muktananda Paramahansa *By Amma*

These and other publications are available at Muktananda Centers
and Ashrams and selected bookstores throughout the world. For further information, contact S.Y.D.A. Foundation, P.O. Box 11071,
Oakland, California 94611 USA. Phone: (415) 655-8677.

Directory

Swami Muktananda has several hundred meditation centers and ashrams throughout the world and many new ones open each month. The list below was accurate as of July 1, 1978. If you cannot locate a center or ashram listed in your area or you are interested in knowing if one has opened in the intervening time, write to S.Y.D.A. Foundation Headquarters, P.O. Box 11071, Oakland, CA 94611, U.S.A. or to any of the major ashrams or major centers which are identified in bold type below. For information on the ashrams and centers in India, contact: Gurudev Siddha Peeth, P.O. Box Ganeshpuri (PIN 401 206), Dist. Thana, Maharashtra, India.

UNITED STATES OF AMERICA

Arizona

Tucson
2905 N. Camino del Oesta
Phone: (602) 743-0462

California

Aptos
215 Elva Dr.
Rio Del Mar
Phone: (408) 688-1665

Big Sur
Esalen Institute
Phone: (415) 667-2335

Bolinas
P.O. Box 243
Programs held at:
165 Elm Rd.
Phone: (415) 868-1098

Campbell
430 East Central
Phone: (408) 378-7491
or 268-2130

Cazadero
P.O. Box 221
No Phone

Corona Del Mar
1701 Oahu Place, Costa Mesa
Programs held at:
430 Carnation Ave.
Phone: (714) 979-8727
or 642-9642

Corte Madera
5 Alta Terr.
Phone: (415) 924-3618

Fremont
41764 Chiltern Dr.
Phone: (415)651-3552

Long Beach
6332 Vermont St.
Phone: (213) 598-5366

Los Angeles (Ashram)
605 S. Mariposa
Phone: (213) 386-2328

Los Gatos
16585 Topping Way
Phone: (408) 356-4421

19330 Overlook Rd.
Phone: (408) 354-1109

Mendocino
1085 Greenwood Rd.
Phone: (707) 895-3130

Oakland (Ashram)
1107 Stanford Ave.
Phone: (415) 655-8677

S.Y.D.A. Foundation
P.O. Box 11071
Oakland, Ca. 94611

8573 Thermal St.
Phone: (415) 638-1161

5662 Chelton Dr.

Occidental
18450 Willow Creek Rd.
Phone: (707) 874-3101

Ojai (Ashram)
P.O. Box 994
Programs held at:
15477 Maricopa Hwy.
Hwy. 33, Ojai Valley
Phone: (805) 646-9111
or 646-1289

401 N Ventura St.
Phone: (805) 646-5228

Palo Alto
476 Ferne
Phone: (415) 494-6914

Redwood City
542 Laurel St.
Phone: (415) 364-9971

Sacramento
1616 21st St.
Phone: (916) 442-6425
& 442-6794

San Diego
1214 Sutter St.
Phone: (714) 295-1617

San Francisco
710 Sanchez St.
Phone: (415) 285-8213

San Jose
7075 Royal Ridge Dr.
Phone: (408) 997-3499

San Rafael
101 Bayview St.
Phone: (415) 456-8511

Santa Cruz
149 Hammond Ave.
Phone: (408) 429-1046

Sherman Oaks
4215 Beverly Glen Blvd.

Colorado

Aspen
307 Francis St.
Phone: (303) 925-4560

Boulder
1355 Chambers Dr.
Phone: (303) 494-1186

2895 E. College #19
Phone: (303) 449-4689

Denver
58 Washington St.
Phone: (303) 733-0360

Pikes Peak
P.O. Box 6311
Colorado Springs
Programs held at:
1331 West Pikes Peak Ave.
Phone: (303) 633-3929

Connecticut

Cornwall
R.F.D. 115
Phone: (203) 672-6797

Greenwich
52 Riversville Rd.
Phone: (203) 531-9310

Litchfield
Box 668
E. Litchfield Rd.
Phone: (203) 567-5395

New Haven
460 Humphrey St.
Phone: (203) 787-2007
Programs held at:
Dwight Hall
Yale University
Phone: (914) 343-8903

Stonington
8 Hancox St.
Phone: (203) 535-3521

Weston-Westport
144 Goodhill Rd.
Weston
Phone: (203) 227-3481

Delaware

Wilmington
5009 Pines Blvd.
Pike Creek Valley
Phone: (302) 239-4290

District of Columbia

Washington D.C.
2900 Connecticut Ave. NW
#326
Programs held at:
4815 Broad Brook Dr.
Bethesda MD
Phone: (202) 244-3319,
483-4849, (301) 530-1009

Florida

Anna Maria Island
P.O. Box L
Bradenton Beach
Programs held at:
2107 Avenue A
Bradenton Beach
Phone: (813) 778-1464

Boca Raton
341 W Camino Real #304
Phone: (305) 368-9258

Fort Walton
419 Corvet St.
Phone: (904) 242-5751

Gainesville (Ashram)
1004 SW First Ave.
Phone: (904) 375-7629

1622 NW 52nd Terr.
Phone: (904) 373-5683

Jacksonville
2130 Dellwood Ave. #1
Phone: (904) 641-3597

Miami
8264 SW 184th Terr.
Phone: (305) 253-3336
& 253-3337

Pensacola
1625 Blvd. Mayor #F4
Phone: (904) 932-9721

Tallahassee
1639 Fernando Dr.
Phone: (305) 224-4282

West Palm Beach
5114 El Claro Dr., S.
Phone: (305) 689-9247

Georgia

Atlanta
1647 N. Rocksprings Rd.
N.E.
Phone: (404) 874-2351

Macon
605 Poplar St.
Phone: (912) 745-6310

Hawaii

Hawaii
P.O. Box 1573
Phone: (808) 955-6264

Honolulu
5660 Haleola St.
Niu Valley
Phone: (808) 373-4881

34 Gartley Pl.
Phone: (808) 595-7073

Lanikai
151 Lanipo Dr.
Phone: (808) 261-0411

Maui
P.O. Box 1813
Phone: (808) 878-1430

Waikiki
Apt. 2144
1777 Ala Moana Blvd.
Phone: (808) 955-6598

Illinois

Aurora
520 North Ave.
Phone: (312) 851-3044

Chicago (Ashram)
2100 W. Bradley Pl.
Phone: (312) 549-7036

P.O. Box 2998
Phone: (312) 929-3893
Programs held at:
917 W. Webster

2422 N. Drake
Phone: (312) 486-6595

468 W. Deming
Phone: (312) 549-5195

Des Plaines
7843 W. Lawrence
Norridge
Programs held at:
750 Cavan La.
Des Plaines
Phone: (312) 453-1186
& 825-0011

Indiana

Indianapolis
5427 Seneca Dr.
Phone: (317) 251-9526

South Bend
733 W. Washington St.
Phone: (219) 287-6147

Kansas

Topeka
7523 Adams RT2
Berryton
Phone: (913) 862-2509

Wichita
3434 Oakland
Phone: (316) 685-5886

Kentucky

Louisville
817 Lyndon La.
Phone: (502) 425-1606

Louisiana

Baton Rouge
3299 Ivanhoe
Phone: (504) 343-6156

New Orleans
5608 Arlene St.
Metairie
Phone: (504) 455-3053

Maryland

Baltimore
P.O. Box 3290
Catonsville
Programs held at:
7204 Fairbrook Rd.
Baltimore
Phone: (301) 747-5236

Catonsville
1906 Rollingwood Rd.
Phone: (301) 744-0652

Massachusetts

Andover
45 Whittier St.
Phone: (617) 475-0966

Boston (Ashram)
301 Waverley Ave.
Newton
Phone: (617)964-3024

Haverhill
1 Arlington Pl.
Phone: (617) 373-1963
& 372-8492

Northampton
25 Franklin St.
Phone: (413) 584-8167

Pepperell
32 Tucker St.
East Pepperell
Phone: (617) 433-9230

Stockbridge
South Lee Road
P.O. Box 793
Phone: (413) 298-4915

Wenham
3 Meridian Rd.
Phone: (617) 468-1311

Michigan

Ann Arbor (Ashram)
902 Baldwin
Phone: (313) 994-5625
& 994-3072

Kalamazoo
1012 Oak St.
Phone: (616) 381-8355

Milan
12925 Whittaker Rd.
Phone: (313) 439-8249

St. Clair
315 Orchard Rd.
Phone: (313) 329-9178

Missouri

Kansas City
5615 Harrison St.
Phone: (816) 363-5276

St. Louis
1722 A Yale
Richmond Hts.
Phone: (314) 781-8706
Programs held at:
4154 Enright
Phone: (314) 652-3374

Montana

Bozeman
804 S. Black
Phone: (406) 587-8825

Nebraska

Scottsbluff
87 Michael
Gering
Phone: (308) 632-2917

New Jersey

Freehold
412 Woody Rd.
Phone: (201) 780-9150

Jersey City
413 Bancroft Hall
509 W. 121st St.
New York NY
Programs held at:
91 Lexington Ave.
Jersey City NJ
Phone: (212) 865-8475

Madison
Central Ave.
Phone: (201) 822-0375

Upper Montclair
489 Highland Ave.
Phone: (201) 783-9261

Warren
6 Casale Dr.
Phone: (201) 647-5769

Whippany
9 Handzel Rd.
Phone: (201) 887-1483

New Mexico

Las Vegas
P.O. Box 3038
Phone: (505) 425-7315

Santa Fe
156 Rendon Rd.
Phone: (505) 983-7652

Rt. 3 Second Village-B
Phone: (505) 982-9529

Rt. 4, Box 50 C
Phone: (505) 988-3639

New York

East Hampton
11 Milina Dr.
Phone: (516) 324-0950

Jamestown
40 Wescott St.
Phone: (716) 485-1428

Mahopac
22 Putnam Professional
Park
Phone: (914) 628-7597

Middletown
118 Monhagen Ave.
(914) 343-2304

Poughkeepsie
2 Barclay St.
Phone: (914) 473-3307

Purchase
Box 1786
State Univ. Purchase
Programs held at:
Room 1021, H & M Bldg.
State Univ. Purchase
Phone: (914) 428-8689

Rochester
291 Pond Road
Honeoye Falls
Phone: (716) 624-3437

Syracuse
865 Ackerman Ave.
Phone: (315) 475-1837
& 422-2890

Yonkers
30 Locust Hill Ave.
Phone: (914) 965-3461

New York City

Brooklyn
169 Greenpoint Ave.
Third Floor
Phone: (212) 389-6058

Manhattan (Ashram)
324 W. 86th St.
Phone: (212) 873-8030

233 W. 83rd St.
Phone: (212) 787-4908

429 East 52nd St.
Phone: (212) 753-4276

115 E. 96th St. #19
Phone: (212) 348-8413
or 628-6094

87-89 Leonard St.
Phone: (212) 925-4718
or 349-2851

10 Stuyvesant Oval #6F
Phone: (212) 777-9219

110 West End Ave. #3E
Phone: (212) 595-2958

Queens
117-14 Union Tpk.
Programs held at:
22 Kew Gardens Rd.
Phone: (212) 268-2248
Programs also held at:
115-25 Metro. Ave. #144
Phone: (212) 268-2248

68-20 Selfridge St. #5F
Phone: (212) 261-9792

Riverdale
4901 Henry Hudson Pkwy.
#5E
Phone: (212) 884-7940

Staten Island
32 Fort Hill Circle
Phone: (212) 273-6460

Ohio

Cincinnati
157 Ridgeview Dr.
Phone: (513) 821-3629

Columbus
173 E. Tompkins
Phone: (614) 268-6739

60

Oklahoma

Norman
1501 Parkview Terr.
No Phone

Oklahoma City
3 S.W. 33rd St.
Phone: (405) 632-1366

2733 NW 15
Phone: (405) 947-6060

Oregon

Eugene
2010 Fairmont Blvd.
Phone: (503) 344-7594

Portland
6027 N.E. 22nd.
Phone: (503) 281-4873

Salem
2995 Perkins Rd. N.E.

Pennsylvania

Erie
3525 Windsor Dr.
Programs held at:
3253 Pine Ave.
Phone: (814) 833-8894

Meshoppen
Box 113

Philadelphia (Ashram)
6429 Wayne Ave.
Phone: (215) 849-0888

Rhode Island

Providence
64 Standish Ave.
Phone: (401) 272-8237

South Carolina

Columbia
312 S. Bull St.
Phone: (803) 771- 6499

South Dakota

Rapid City
1916 Hillview Dr.
Programs held at:
1525 Forest Court
Phone: (605) 342-6109

Tennessee

Oak Ridge
712 S. Main St.
Clinton
Phone: (615) 457-2203

Memphis
810 Washington Ave.
Apt. 803

Texas

Dallas (Ashram)
208 McKinney
Richardson
Phone: (214) 690-6736

Dripping Springs
Star Rt. 1-B, Box 92
Phone: (512) 858-7045

Houston
1640 Harvard
Phone: (713) 862-8411
& 443-6587

811 Branard St.
Phone: (713) 529-0006
& 667-2241

Vermont

Chester
P.O. Box 22
Phone: (802) 875-3412

Virginia

Louisa
P.O. Box 545
Phone: (703) 967-0274

Norfolk
749 W. Princess Anne Rd.
Phone: (804) 625-9379

Roanoke
3534 Hershberger Rd. NW
Phone: (703) 563-5905

Washington

Bellingham
2908 Lincoln St.
Phone: (206) 676-0543

Bremerton
2509 E. Phinney Bay Dr.
Phone: (206) 377-2046

Mercer Island
2815 67th S.E.
Phone: (206) 232-1575

Richland
2304 Enterprise Dr.
Phone: (509) 946-7573

Seattle
3721 Meridian Ave. N.
Phone: (206) 632-1484

15709 25th S.W.
Phone: (206) 242-1151

6006 2nd Ave., N.W.
Phone: (206) 782-2027

Spokane
1835 E. 14th Ave.
Phone: (509) 535-2837

Walla Walla
210 Marcus St.
Phone: (509) 527-5488

Wisconsin

Madison
4150 Hiawatha Dr.
Phone: (414) 922-6518

Wauwatosa
7810 Harwood Ave.
Phone: (414) 476-1718

AFRICA

South Africa

P.O. Box 42282
42a Clare Rd.
Fordsburg, Johannesburg
Programs held at:
4631 Lily Ave.
Extension 3 Lenasia

ASIA

Israel

Holon
14 Hararee St.
Phone: (03) 846 385

Shenkin 46, 3rd Entrance
Givataim Israel 53304
Phone: 03-281221, 281222
& 281223 (At work)

Philippines

PSC #1 Box 2295
APO San Francisco CA
96286 USA
Programs held at:
Building 275
Clark Air Force Base
Angeles City Philippines
Phone: 20119

Australia

Armidale
Puddledock Rd.
Armidale NSW 2350

Bung Bong (Ashram)
P.O. Box 77
Avoca VIC 3467

Canberra
5 Mackellar Crescent
Cook, Canberra ACT 2614
Phone: 512 803 (after
6 pm) & (work) 062 89 6379

Ferny Creek
Wondoora, School Rd.
Ferny Creek, Melbourne
3786 VIC

Hawthorn
313 Auburn Rd., Hawthorn
Melbourne VIC 3122
Phone: 82 1985

Kalamunda
54 Kalamunda Rd.
Kalamunda 6076 WA

Melbourne (Ashram)
66 George St., Fitzroy
Melbourne VIC 3065
Phone: 419 6950

Narnargoon
Olsen Rd.
N. Narnargoon VIC 3182
Phone: (STD) 059 42 8206

Perth
P.O. Box 158
Cottesloe WA 6011
Programs held at:
9 Ailie St.
Peppermint Grove WA
Phone: 384-4600

Sydney
33 Walker St.
North Sydney NSW 2060
Phone: 929 5431 &
(work) 290 2199

Townsville
5 Morehead St., Flat #1
S. Townsville QLD 4810

Victoria
The Patch
Lot 1 Kallista Emerald Rd.
Victoria 3792
Phone: 756-7009

New Zealand

Auckland
43 A Ranfurly Rd.
Epsom, Auckland

Dunedin
82 Gladstone Rd.
Dunedin, South Island

Canada

Malton
7566 Wrenwood Crescent
Malton ONT L4T 2V7
Phone: (416) 677-3301

Mississauga
6789 Segovia Rd.
Mississauga ONT L5N 1P1
Phone: (416) 826-4512

Ottawa
1300 Pinecrest #1605
Ottawa ONT
Phone: (613) 828-7214

Peterborough
327 Charlotte St.
Peterborough ONT K9J 7C3
Phone: (705) 652-3386

Timmins
107 Pine N.
Timmins ONT P4N 6K8
Phone: (705) 267-5776

Toronto
48 Dundonald St.
Toronto ONT M4Y 1K2
Phone: (416) 923-5402

Vancouver
P.O. Box 2990
Vancouver BC V6B 3X4
Phone: (604) 274-9008
& 738-2032

Victoria
1525 McRae Ave.
Phone: (604) 598-2173

EUROPE

England

United Kingdom
91 Taybridge Rd.
London SW 11
Phone: 01-228-0969

Clapham
91 Taybridge Rd.
London SW 11
Phone: 01-228-0969

Eastborne
30 Oakhurst Rd.
Eastborne, Sussex
Phone: Eastborne 37028

Hounslow
15 Ivanhoe Rd.
Hounslow West, Middlesex
Phone: 01-572-3432

Ilford
358 Thorold Rd.
Ilford, Essex
Phone: 01-554-8112
01-552-2200

London
47 Maclean Rd.
Forest Hill, London SE23

82, Livingstone Rd.
Walthamstow
London E17, 9AX
Phone: 01-521-5269

Lowestoft
28 Southwell Rd.
Lowestoft, Suffolk
NR33 ORN
Phone: 05-026-0793

Surrey
Coxhill House
Chobham, Surrey GU24 8AU
Phone: Chobham 8926

France

Bourbourg
12, Ave. General Leclerc
F. 59630
Phone: (16) 20.68.12.91

Nice
30 rue Marceau
Nice 06

Paris
8 rue Freycinet
75116 Paris France
Programs held at:
146 rue Raymond
Losserand
75014 Paris
Phone: 720-8430

33 Ave. du Chateau de Bertin
78400 Chatoux
Programs held at:
14 rue des Sts. Peres
Paris 75007
Phone: 976--7004

Vesoul
26 Bld. des Allies
Vesoul 70 000

Italy

Rome
Via Ara Delle Rose, 290
Santa Cornelia, Km 3
Phone: (06) 691-3605

Netherlands

Amsterdam
Weteringschans 75
1017 RX Amsterdam
Phone: 020-23.29.92

Soest
Ereprijsstraat 49
Phone: 02155-1717

Spain

Barcelona
Ferrer Vidal 8
Manresa

Madrid
Espana
General Pardinas 21
Madrid 1
Phone: 275-3239

Sweden

Malmö
S. Forstadsgat. 102a 3v
S-214 20 Malmö
Phone: (040) 130862

Stockholm
Surbrunnsgatan 6
S-114 21 Stockholm
Phone: (08) 435709

Switzerland

Bern
Brunngasse 54, 3011

Geneva
49, Cure-Baud
1212 Grand-Lancy/Geneva
Phone: 94 79 56

West Germany

Darup
Roruperstr. 5

Frankfurt
Fischergasse 5
6050 Offenbach 8
Phone: 0611861260

Munich
Lieberweg 12
D-8000 Munchen 45

Querschied
Am Moosberg 8
(near Saarbrucken)

Mexico

Guadalajara
Av. Americas 1485
Guadalajara 6
Phone: 41-11-35

Mexico City (Ashram)
Apartado 41-890
Mexico 10 DF
Programs held at:
Euclides 9
Colonia Nva. Anzures
Mexico 5 DF
Phone: (905) 545-9375

San Jeronimo
Cerrada Presa 28
San Jeronimo 20
Phone: 595-0980

Tepic
Guerrero 74 Ote.
Tepic, Nayarit
Phone: Tepic 2-27-52

SOUTH AMERICA

Curacao
P.O. Box 807
Curacao Netherlands
Antilles
Phone: 35251, 12213,
&11769

Kwartje 39 Sta. Rosa
Willemstad, Curacao
Netherlands Antilles
Phone: 38880

Trinidad
Union Village, Claxton
Bay
Trinidad West Indies

INDIA

Andhra Pradesh — 1

HYDERABAD

Shree Gurudev Center
Shri Rameshchandra Sanghani,
Shri Bakul Seth,
"Muktashram"
% Shri Pravinchandra Modi,
6-3-344 Jubilee Hills,
Hyderabad — 34

Delhi — 3

Siddha Yoga Dham,
Shri Balram Nanda,
Shri Ramesh Kapur,
M-11, Mukta Niwas, Green Park Extn.
New Delhi — 110016

Siddha Yoga Dhyan Kendra,
Shri Santram Vatsya,
K-47, Navin Shahdara, Delhi — 32

Shree Muktanand Dhyan Mandir,
Smt. Urmila Saxena,
Shri Parmama Shanker,
193-E, Dev Nagar,
New Delhi — 110005

Gujarat — 20

AHMEDABAD

Shree Muktanand Dhyan Kendra,
Shri Shirishbhai Desai,
Kum. Bhavna Dhora,
424, Hariniwas, Ashram Road,
Opp. La Gajjar Chamber,
Ahmedabad — 380009

Shree Gurudev Dhyan Kendra,
Shri Niranjan Mehta,
Shri Mahendrabhai Shukla,
15 August Bunglow,
Near Old Police Chawky, Maninagar,
Ahmedabad — 380008

Shree Gurudev Dhyan Mandir,
Smt. Kokila J. Parikh,
5B- Motisagar Society,
Narayan Nagar Road, Paldi,
Ahmedabad — 380007

Shree Gurudev Dhyan Kendra,
Shri Shriram Modak,
A/2 Minita Apartments, Near Swati Soc.
St. Xaviers High School Road,
Navarangpura, Ahmedabad — 380014

ATUL

Shree Gurudev Dhyan Kendra,
Shri Surendra H. Bhatt,
Shri Ramnikbhai Raval,
Room No — 26, A type Colony,
Atul, Dist.-Valsad

VALSAD (BULSAR)

Shree Gurudev Dhyan Kendra,
Dr. Ratubhai Desai,
Sandhya, Shree Buddha Society,
Halar Road, Valsad

Shree Gurudev Dhyan Mandir,
Shri Dilipbhai Desai,
Smt. Darpanaben Desai,
Hanuman Bhagda, Valsad.

Shree Gurudev Dhyan Mandir,
Dr. Jitubhai Parekh,
Kum. Laxmiben Prajapati,
Gangotri, Dhobivad, Valsad

DAHOD

Shree Muktanand Dhyan Kendra,
Shri Gopaldas K. Panchal,
138 'L' Satrasta, Opp. Dayanand Hindi
School, Freelandgang, Dahod
Dist.-Panchmahal

HIMATNAGAR

Shree Gurudev Dhyan Kendra,
Shri Kishorilal Sharma,
Smt. Chandrakantaben Jani,
Kum. Maya Mehta,
Sharma Cottage, Polo Ground,
Near L.I.C. Office, Himatnagar - 383001

KUKARWADA

Siddha Yoga Dham,
Dr. Gangadhar Patel,
Mahant Prempuriji Maharaj,
Kukarwada, Taluke — Vijapur,
Dist.-Mehsana

MOTA JOOJVA

Shree Gurudev Dhyan Kendra,
Shri Babubhai C. Patel,
Shri Dayaji D. Patel,
Shri Thakur D. Patel,
Mota Joojava, Dist.-Valsad

MOTA PONDHA

Shree Gurudev Dhyan Kendra,
Shri Prabhubhai D. Patel,
Mota Pondha, Via- Vapi,
Dist.-Valsad

PARNERA PARDI

Shree Gurudev Dhyan Kendra,
Shri Dolatrai G. Desai,
Parnera Pardi, Dist.-Valsad

SAMANI

Shree Gurudev Dhyan Mandir,
Shri Ghanshyambhai Patel,
Smt. Vidyaben Patel,
At/Post- Samani, Tal.- Amod,
Dist.-Bharuch

SURAT

Siddha Yoga Dham,
Shri Bachubhai Wadiwala,
Smt. Urmila Jariwala,
Shree Nityanand Bhavan,
Kelapith, Surat

UKAI

Shree Gurudev Dhyan Mandir,
Shri Jayantibhai L. Desai,
3A/32 Bhuriwel Colony
Ukai, Dist.-Surat

VAPI

Shree Gurudev Dhyan Mandir,
Shri Krishnarao Dhonde,
Rang Kripa, Zanda Chowk,
Vapi — 396191

DAMAN

Shree Gurudev Dhyan Kendra,
Shri Chunilal Patel,
Bhardwaj Kutir,
Ramji Mandir Compound, Wadi Falia,
Nani Daman, Via- Vapi

SELVASSA

Shree Gurudev Dhyan Mandir,
Shri Madhubhai Patel,
Matruchhaya, Muktanand Marg,
Selvassa, (Dadra Nagar Haveli)

Madhya Pradesh — 3

INDORE

Siddha Yoga Dhyan Kendra,
Shri Basant Kumar Joshi,
89, Emli Bazar (Lal Makan),
Indore — 452002

MHOW

Swami Muktanand Bhakta Mandal,
Shri Balwantrai Sharma,
Bunglow No. L/4A. Rly. Colony,
Mhow, Dist. Indore

RATLAM

Shree Sadguru Bhakta Mandal,
Shri Chunilal Rathod,
Shri Jaisinh S. Pol,
Sadguru Dhyan Kutir,
Nagar Nigam Colony, Block No. 316,
Gandhi Nagar, Ratlam

Maharashtra — 14

AURANGABAD

Muktanand Dhyan Kendra,
Shri B.S. Patil,
Smt. Rajani Patil,
Mukteswari, Prabhat Colony,
Aurangabad

BARAMATI

Shree Gurudev Dhyan Kendra,
Smt. Lila Kale,
Kale Wada, Baramati,
Dist.-Poona

BHUSAWAL

Shree Gurudev Mandir,
Shri Sudhir Rajabhao Kulkarni,
Muktanand Bhavan, Ram Mandir
Bhusawal, Dist.-Jalgaon

BOMBAY

Siddha Yoga Dhyan Kendra,
Kum. Bharati Dicholkar,
New Liberty Co. Op. Housing Society,
Guru Kripa, Block No. 9,
Liberty Garden Cross Road No. 4,
Malad, Bombay — 400065

Nityamukta Siddha Yoga Dham,
Shri Pranubhai Desai,
A/17 Madhav Apartments,
Shimpoli, Borivli, (West) Bombay

Siddha Yoga Dhyan Kendra,
Kum. Lalita Parasarmani,
Guru Chhaya, 62/1 Mulund Colony,
Mulund, Bombay — 400082

DOMBIVALI

Shree Sadguru Muktanand
Swadhyaya Mandal,
Shri Vasantrao Malpathak,
Khot Kaparekar Bldg.,
Agarkar Road, Dombivali (East)
Dist.-Thana

FAIZPUR

Shree Gurudev Dhyan Mandir,
Shri Shamlal Varma,
Shri Rajendrakumar Varma,
Faizpur, Dist.-Jalgaon

KOLHAPUR

Siddha Yoga Dhyan Kendra,
Smt. Jayashree Kori,
Smt. Vijaya D. Ligade,
Prabha, Rajarampuri,
14th Street, Kolhapur — 416001

MANMAD

Shree Gurudev Dhyan Kendra,
Smt. Kusumatai D. Deshmukh,
Railway Colony, R.B. 2-629A,
Yeola Road, Manmad

NAGPUR

Siddha Yoga Dhyan Kendra,
Shri Vasantrao Ghonge,
Mukta Niwas, Gopalnagar,
Nagpur — 440010

POONA

Shree Gurudev Dhyan Mandir,
Prof. G. H. Sujan,
44 Connought House,
12 Sadhu Vasvani Road,
Poona — 411001

Siddha Yoga Dhyan Mandir,
Smt. Pragna Trivedi,
"Kamal", 479/2 Harekrishna Path,
Shivaji Nagar, Poona — 411016

SAPTASHRING

Shree Saptashring Gurudev Ashram,
Swami Prakashanand Saraswati,
Saptashring Gadh,
Post- Nanduri, Tal.-Kalvan,
Dist.-Nasik,
(Residential Ashram)

Rajasthan — 4

JAIPUR

Shree Muktanand Dhyan Mandir,
Smt. Bhagvati Mukta,
B-222, Janata Colony, Agra Road,
Jaipur — 302008

Shree Muktanand Dhyan Mandir,
Shri Nandkishor Varma,
Shree Muktanand Niketan,
Gator Road, Brahmapuri,
Jaipur — 302002

NAGAUR

Siddha Yoga Dhyan Kendra,
Shri Sitaram Soni,
Katharia Bazar, Nagaur

TONK

Shree Muktanand Dhyan Mandir,
Shri Gopalsimh Bhati,
Abdul Qayum's House,
Barmor Darwaja, Tonk

Uttar Pradesh — 2

AGRA

Siddah Yoga Dhyan Kendra,
Dr. Chandrapal Singh,
Ram Niwas, 32 Heerabag Colony,
Swamibag, Agra — 282005

TENTI GAON

Shree Muktanand Dhyan Kendra,
Shri Ramshankar Lavania,
At/Post- Tenti Gaon, Dist.-Mathura

West Bangal — 2

CALCUTTA

Muktanand Dhyan Kendra,
Shri Balkrishna Agarwal,
11 Pollack Street, 1st Floor,
Room No.-3, Calcutta — 700001

Muktanand Dhyan Kendra,
Smt. Shukla Lal,
Shri Shadi Lal,
Flat No. 15, 8th Floor,
8-B, Alipur Road, Calcutta - 700027